my **revision** notes

OCR AS and A-Level History

DEMOCRACY AND DICTATORSHIPS IN GERMANY
1919–1963

Nick Fellows

HODDER
EDUCATION
AN HACHETTE UK COMPANY

Every effort has been made to trace all copyright holders, but if any have been inadvertently overlooked, the Publishers will be pleased to make the necessary arrangements at the first opportunity.

Although every effort has been made to ensure that website addresses are correct at time of going to press, Hodder Education cannot be held responsible for the content of any website mentioned in this book. It is sometimes possible to find a relocated web page by typing in the address of the home page for a website in the URL window of your browser.

Hachette UK's policy is to use papers that are natural, renewable and recyclable products and made from wood grown in sustainable forests. The logging and manufacturing processes are expected to conform to the environmental regulations of the country of origin.

Orders: please contact Bookpoint Ltd, 130 Milton Park, Abingdon, Oxon OX14 4SE. Telephone: +44 (0)1235 827720. Fax: +44 (0)1235 400454. Email education@bookpoint.co.uk Lines are open from 9 a.m. to 5 p.m., Monday to Saturday, with a 24-hour message answering service. You can also order through our website: www.hoddereducation.co.uk

ISBN: 978 1 4718 7585 4

© Nick Fellows 2017

First published in 2017 by

Hodder Education,
An Hachette UK Company
Carmelite House
50 Victoria Embankment
London EC4Y 0DZ

www.hoddereducation.co.uk

Impression number   10 9 8 7 6 5 4 3 2 1

Year   2020 2019 2018 2017

Cover photo © chriszwaenepoel – Fotolia
Illustrations by Integra
Typeset by Integra Software Services Pvt. Ltd., Pondicherry, India
Printed in India

A catalogue record for this title is available from the British Library.

My revision planner

4 Divided Germany: the Federal Republic and the DDR, 1949–63

Introduction

Unit 2: Non-British Period Study

Component 2 involves the study of a period of non-British history and at AS Level will also involve the evaluation of a historical interpretation from one of two named topics. The type of essay set for both AS and A-Level is similar, but the AS mark scheme does not have a Level 6 (see page vii).

Germany: Democracy and Dictatorships in Germany 1919–1963

The specification lists the content of Democracy and Dictatorships under four key topics.

Key topic 1 – The establishment and development of the Weimar Republic, 1919 to January 1933

Key topic 2 – The establishment of the Nazi dictatorship and its domestic policies, February 1933 to 1939

Key topic 3 – The impact of war and defeat on Germany, 1939–49

Key topic 4 – Divided Germany: the Federal Republic and the DDR, 1949–63

Although each period of study is set out in chronological sections in the specification, an exam question may arise from one or more of these sections.

AS Level

The AS examination which you may be taking includes all the content.

You are required to answer:

Section A: ONE question from a choice of TWO. This is a traditional essay and will require you to use your knowledge to explain, analyse and assess key features of the period studied and then reach a judgement about the issue in the question. The question is worth 30 marks.

Section B: ONE interpretation question. The specification names the two key topics from which the interpretation will be drawn. Questions will require candidates to evaluate the strengths and limitations of a given historical interpretation, in the form of either one or two sentences, by applying your own knowledge and awareness of the debate to the given interpretation. The question is worth 20 marks.

The exam lasts one and a half hours, and you are advised to spend slightly more time on Section A.

At AS Level, Unit 2 will be worth a total of 50 marks and 50 per cent of the AS examination.

A-Level

The A-Level examination at the end of the course includes all the content.

You are required to answer ONE question with TWO parts from a choice of TWO questions.

Each question will have TWO parts. Question (a) will be a short essay in which you are asked to analyse two issues and reach a judgement as to which is the more important or significant. Question (b) is a traditional period study essay and will require you to use your knowledge to explain, analyse and assess key features of the period studied and then reach a judgement about the issue in the question.

The short essay is worth 10 marks and the traditional essay is worth 20 marks.

The two parts of each question will be drawn from different parts of the specification.

The exam lasts for one hour. You should spend about 20 minutes on question (a) and 40 minutes on question (b).

At A-Level, Unit 2 will be worth a total of 30 marks and 15 per cent of the A-Level examination.

In both the AS and A-Level examinations you are being tested on your ability to:
- use relevant historical information
- analyse factors and reach a judgement.
- In the AS examination you are also being tested on your ability to analyse and evaluate the different ways in which aspects of the past have been interpreted.

How to use this book

This book has been designed to help you develop the knowledge and skills necessary to succeed in the examination.

The book is divided into four sections – one for each section of the AS and A-Level specifications.

Each section is made up of a series of topics organised into double-page spreads.

On the left-hand page you will find a summary of the key content you will need to learn.

Words in bold in the key content are defined in the glossary (see pages 88–90).

On the right-hand page you will find exam-focused activities.

Together, these two strands of the book will provide you with the knowledge and skills essential for examination success.

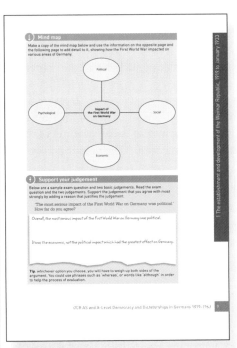

Examination activities

There are three levels of exam-focused activities:
- Band 1 activities are designed to develop the foundation skills needed to pass the exam. These have a green heading and this symbol:
- Band 2 activities are designed to build on the skills developed in Band 1 activities and to help you to achieve a C grade. These have an orange heading and this symbol:
- Band 3 activities are designed to enable you to access the highest grades. These have a purple heading and this symbol:

Some of the activities have answers or suggested answers on pages 93–6. These have the following symbol to indicate this:

Each section ends with exam-style questions and sample answers with commentary. This will give you guidance on what is expected to achieve the top grade.

You can also keep track of your revision by ticking off each topic heading in the book, or by ticking the checklist on the contents page. Tick each box when you have:

- revised and understood a topic
- completed the activities.

Mark schemes

For some of the activities in the book it will be useful to refer to the mark schemes for this paper. Below are abbreviated forms.

AS Level

Level	Essay	Interpretation
5	Mostly focused, supported answer, with good analysis and evaluation to reach a supported judgement. (25–30)	Very good analysis of the interpretation, aware of the debate and uses detailed knowledge to evaluate the strengths and limitations. (17–20)
4	Some focus, with support and analysis with limited evaluation and judgement. (19–24)	Good analysis of the interpretation, some awareness of the debate and uses knowledge to evaluate the strengths and limitations. (13–16)
3	Partial focus on the question, with some knowledge and analysis, but little or no judgement. (13–18)	Partial analysis of the interpretation, some knowledge and awareness of the debate. May be limited in treatment of strength or limitations. (9–12)
2	Focus is descriptive and may be more on the topic than the question. Any analysis may be implied. (7–12)	Limited analysis, may describe the interpretation and the debate. Any evaluation is implied or superficial. (5–8)
1	Focus on the topic and attempts at analysis will be little more than assertion. (1–6)	Focused more on the topic than the given interpretation. Knowledge is general and evaluation is asserted. (1–4)

A-Level

Level	Short-answer essay	Essay
6	Analyses and evaluates both factors with detailed knowledge to reach a developed judgement. (9–10)	Well-focused, supported answer, with very good analysis and developed evaluation to reach a supported and sustained judgement. (17–20)
5	Analyses and evaluates both factors with some knowledge to reach a developed judgement. (7–8)	Mostly focused, supported answer with good analysis and evaluation to reach a supported judgement. (13–16)
4	Some analysis and evaluation of both factors, with some support and judgement. (5–6)	Some focus, with support and analysis with limited evaluation and judgement. (10–12)
3	Partial analysis and evaluation, with some knowledge to reach a basic judgement. (3–4)	Partial focus on the question, with some knowledge and analysis, but little or no judgement. (7–9)
2	Limited analysis and knowledge, with a simple judgement. (2)	Focus is descriptive and may be more on the topic than the question. Any analysis may be implied. (4–6)
1	General analysis and knowledge with assertion. (1)	Focus on the topic and attempts at analysis will be little more than assertion. (1–3)

1 The establishment and development of the Weimar Republic, 1919 to January 1933

The consequences of the First World War

The First World War, which began in 1914, had split Europe into two armed camps, with Germany, Austria–Hungary and Turkey (the Central Powers) fighting against Britain, France and Russia (the Allies). Russia made peace with Germany in 1917, but the USA joined the Allies. In order to try to defeat the Allies before large numbers of American troops arrived, Germany launched a massive attack against Allied forces in France in the spring of 1918. At first this was very successful, but war-weariness and the strength of the Allies brought it to a halt. On 29 September, the chief of staff, General Ludendorff, informed his superior, Field Marshal **Paul von Hindenburg**, and Chancellor Hertling that the war was lost and that Germany should appeal to the USA for an **armistice**. Ludendorff urged the creation of a more democratic regime to show that Germany was serious about making peace.

Impact on the German people

News of impending defeat in late October/early November 1918 was a shock, despite the increasing food shortages caused by the naval blockade, as Germany had defeated Russia, and German troops were still in Northern France and Belgium. During the war the army commanders had been telling the people that they were close to victory.

The navy disagreed with an armistice and ordered the fleet to sea, but this led to a mutiny, which was followed by the establishment of soviets in many cities across Germany.

Political impact

On 9 November the **Kaiser** abdicated. Power went to a Council of People's Representatives, a temporary government under **Friedrich Ebert**, the leader of the largest political party, the **SPD**, until a national assembly could be elected. It appeared as if Germany was on the verge of revolution.

Ebert and the SPD did not want a revolution like in Russia because it would:
- lead to civil war
- disrupt demobilisation
- disrupt the distribution of food
- hinder peace negotiations.

Ebert was able to prevent a revolution for the following reasons:
- He maintained the support of the army by not reforming it or creating a new force.
- He kept the support of industrialists, who negotiated with trade unions the Central Working Association Agreement, which gave workers an eight-hour day and established workers' councils in large companies.
- The working class was divided between the communists (KPD), who wanted a Soviet style of government, and supporters of the SPD, who wanted a parliamentary system.

Economic impact

The war had a considerable economic impact on Germany, with the following results when it ended in 1918:
- Industrial production was only two-thirds that of 1913.
- National income was one-third that of 1913.
- There were 600,000 widows and 2 million children without fathers, with the result that by 1925 the state was spending one-third of its budget on war pensions.

Social impact

The war deepened divisions within German society, with huge gaps in the living standards between rich and poor. This situation had been made worse by the restrictions placed on workers' earnings during the war, while factory owners had been able to make large profits. During the war, many women had worked in factories and some believed that this had damaged family values.

The establishment of a republic

Following the Kaiser's abdication, Ebert signed an armistice and announced that the Republic would guarantee:
- freedom of speech
- freedom of worship
- better working conditions.

A new constitution was drawn up, but the change in government from an autocratic system to a new democratic government created opposition and challenges (see page 12). This helped to create the **'stab-in-the-back' myth**, which claimed that Germany had been betrayed by politicians such as Ebert and that it was this that prevented Germany from winning the war.

Mind map

Make a copy of the mind map below and use the information on the opposite page and the following page to add detail to it, showing how the First World War impacted on various areas of Germany.

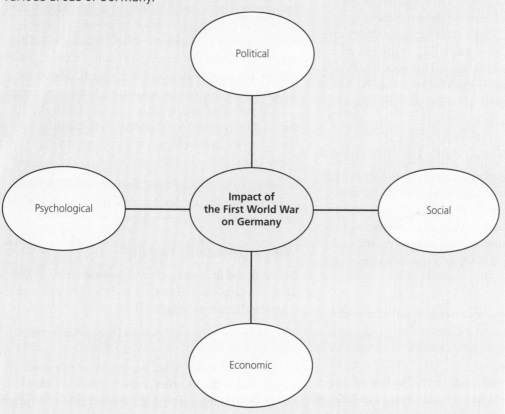

Support your judgement

Below are a sample exam question and two basic judgements. Read the exam question and the two judgements. Support the judgement that you agree with most strongly by adding a reason that justifies the judgement.

'The most serious impact of the First World War on Germany was political.' How far do you agree?

Overall, the most serious impact of the First World War on Germany was political.

_____

_____

It was the economic, not the political impact which had the greatest effect on Germany.

_____

_____

Tip: whichever option you choose, you will have to weigh up both sides of the argument. You could use phrases such as 'whereas', or words like 'although', in order to help the process of evaluation.

The impact of the Treaty of Versailles

Given the military position of Germany at the end of the war, the government hoped that it would be able to negotiate a moderate peace so that it would be able to recover its strength. Germany did not want to pay **reparations**, apart from the cost of damage in Northern France and Belgium, but it was willing to give up Alsace-Lorraine and some land in Poland. However, it expected Austria and other German-speaking regions to be able to join Germany. Germany expected to join the **League of Nations** and remain a great power.

The terms of the Treaty of Versailles

With the **Treaty of Versailles**, Germany lost 10 per cent of its land, 12.5 per cent of its population, 16 per cent of its coal and 48 per cent of its iron industry, as well as all its colonies. It was also weakened militarily, and had to accept guilt for starting the war and pay reparations, effectively destroying its position as a great power.

Land lost

- Upper Silesia, which contained coal and steel works
- Much of West Prussia and Posen
- Schleswig, which was given a **plebiscite** on whether to return to Denmark
- Alsace-Lorraine, which was returned to France, and Eupen and Malmedy, which were returned to Belgium
- The **Saar**, which was placed under the control of the League of Nations for 15 years
- The Rhineland, which was to be occupied by Allied forces for 15 years.

Military reductions

- The army was reduced to 100,000 men.
- The navy was reduced to 15,000 men.
- The General Staff was disbanded.
- Germany was not allowed tanks, aircraft, submarines or poison gas.
- The number of ships was limited.

Reparations

At the time of Versailles, it was not known how much damage had been caused, which led to the establishment of the Reparations Commission to investigate how much Germany could afford. The Commission did not report until 1921. The figure was finally fixed at £6,600 million, but some was to be paid in goods. The ability of Germany to pay has caused debate: Germany claimed it could not afford to pay, while historians have argued that it could, and that the demands were less than the punishment it gave to Russia at the **Treaty of Brest-Litovsk**.

In order to justify punishing Germany, the 'War Guilt' clause (Clause 231) declared that Germany was guilty of starting the war.

Was the treaty harsh?

Germany had little choice but to sign the treaty, as the naval blockade was still in force and the Allies were in the Rhineland, ready to invade.

The seizure of industrial lands and the loss of colonies made it harder for Germany to pay the reparations. Many Germans lived under Allied occupation, while others were forced to live in other countries, such as Poland. Most Germans disapproved of the treaty; the government lost support by signing it; and it created long-term bitterness.

However, the treaty was not as harsh as it appears. German views that they had not lost the war meant that no matter what treaty had been signed there would have been opposition. The creation of new, smaller states in Central Europe also meant that Germany was still the strongest power there, and as **Gustav Stresemann** would show, it could soon recover (see page 14).

(i) Turning assertion into argument

Below are a sample question and a series of assertions. Read the exam question and then add a justification to each of the assertions to turn each one into an argument.

'The Treaty of Versailles was harsh on Germany'. How far do you agree?

The Treaty of Versailles was harsh on Germany economically and territorially because

_____

_____

However, it did not completely reduce Germany's influence in Europe because

_____

_____

Nevertheless, it was still a cause of bitterness as

_____

_____

(!) Delete as applicable

Below are a sample exam question and a paragraph written in answer to this question. Read the paragraph and decide which of the options (in bold) is the most appropriate. Delete the least appropriate options and complete the paragraph by justifying your selection.

'The Treaty of Versailles did little damage to Germany'. How far do you agree?

It is **fair/unfair** to argue that the Treaty of Versailles did little damage to Germany. The territorial losses were **great/limited/minimal** and had **great/limited/minimal** impact on the economy. It did mean that **many/some/few** Germans were now living outside the borders of Germany. In some ways the loss of colonies had a **greater/lesser** impact on the economy. However, the government **gained/lost** support for signing the treaty and this would make it **harder/easier** for it to survive the challenges it faced. It was not just the loss of land that the government had to deal with, but military issues. The military reductions had **great/limited/minimal impact** as Germany felt **secure/insecure** from the threat from France. In this way, to a **great/limited** extent Versailles was damaging for Germany.

_____

_____

The challenges to Weimar, 1919–23

Many German people wanted the return of the Kaiser, and the new republic was unpopular from the very beginning, with its position further weakened by the signing of the Treaty of Versailles. The period from 1919 to 1923 was one of continuous crisis and this further damaged the reputation of the Republic. The economic and social legacy of the war (see page 8) only added to the problems of the Republic.

The Weimar Constitution

Some have argued that the constitution weakened the Republic as it created instability.

There were three key elements to the constitution:
- The **president** was directly elected by universal franchise; he chose the **chancellor** and could declare a state of emergency.
- The Reichsrat was the upper house, where individual states were represented.
- The **Reichstag** was the lower house, elected by universal franchise and on the basis of **proportional representation**. This system allowed many small parties to gain representation and meant that governments were **coalitions**, which were subject to frequent change.

There were also many parties, such as the right-wing **DNVP**, that were opposed to the **Weimar** democracy.

The challenges from the left

Many workers had hoped for the establishment of a series of soviets, factory councils and the **nationalisation** of industry, but these hopes did not materialise. The decision to give power to parliament and the lack of reforms led to the resignation of the Independent Socialists from the Council of People's Representatives, and to the formation of the Communist Party (KPD).

The KPD attempted to seize power, through the **Spartacist Revolt**, in Berlin in January 1919. Karl Liebknecht and Rosa Luxemburg, two of its leaders, were murdered and the revolt was put down by the **Freikorps**.

There were further challenges from the left and soviets were set up in Munich and Bremen. However, these were also crushed. An uprising also broke out in the **Ruhr** in March 1920 and the KPD soon controlled much of the region. This was crushed by the *Freikorps*.

The challenges from the right

Many extreme parties emerged on the right, most notably the **German Workers' Party**, whose meetings **Hitler** attended. The major challenge to Weimar came from the **Kapp Putsch** in March 1920, led by **Wolfgang Kapp**, the founder of the German Fatherland Party, following government attempts to disband the *Freikorps*. It was defeated by trade unions calling a general strike, which paralysed public services.

The crisis of 1923

The occupation of the Ruhr

In January 1923, Germany fell behind in its reparation payments and France and Belgium occupied the Ruhr. This united Germany; reparation payments were halted and workers in the Ruhr went on strike. This put pressure on the economy and added to inflation, made worse by the government printing money to pay the strikers. The French brought in their own workers and this increased tensions further.

Hyperinflation

The war had caused inflation in Germany, but by printing more money to pay the strikers and compensate for lost tax revenues, the value of the mark fell so that it was worthless. This destroyed savings and ruined those on **fixed incomes**. Prices rose so fast that the **black market** and **barter** flourished. Some, such as industrialists, did gain from this situation.

Munich Putsch

Bavaria was governed by a conservative Catholic regime. It wanted to unite the nationalist right, which included the Nazi Party, to restore traditional values. Despite some opposition, the plan was for a **putsch** in Munich and then a march on Berlin. Hitler acted and seized the Bavarian state governor. After initial success, it was defeated by police. Sixteen Nazis and three police were killed; Hitler was arrested, put on trial and sentenced to imprisonment for five years, but was released after just nine months.

Why did Weimar survive?

There were other political murders during this period:
- Karl Gareis, leader of the USPD (Independent Social Democratic Party of Germany)
- Matthias Erzberger
- Walter Rathenau, the foreign minister.

Yet the Republic survived for a number of reasons:
- The government took effective action.
- Many in Germany were willing to give Weimar a chance.
- Political opposition was weaker than it appeared.

ⓘ Introducing an argument

Below are a sample exam question, a list of key points to be made in the essay, and a simple introduction and conclusion for the essay. Read these and then, using the information on the opposite page, rewrite the introduction and the conclusion in order to develop an argument.

Assess the reasons why there was unrest in Germany in the period 1919–23.

Key points:

- Threat from both the left and right wings
- Economic difficulties
- Abdication of the Kaiser and dislike of the new government
- Treaty of Versailles
- Weak government.

Introduction:

There were many reasons why there was unrest in Germany in the period from the end of the First World War to 1923. These reasons are linked to politics, economics and the impact of the war. It is important to consider the situation in Germany at the end of the First World War because the new government inherited many problems. All of these factors help to explain why there was so much unrest in the period 1919–23.

Conclusion:

To conclude, there were many reasons why there was unrest in the period 1919–23. These reasons were linked to the economic problems after the war, as well as to politics and the impact of defeat in the war. The context of the defeat in the war was also important. However, the most important reason was dislike of the new government.

ⓘ Spectrum of importance

Below are a sample exam question and a list of general points which could be used to answer the question. Use your own knowledge, and the information on the page opposite and from earlier in the book, to reach a judgement about the seriousness of the problems faced by Weimar in the period from the end of the First World War to 1923. Write the numbers on the spectrum below to indicate their relative seriousness. Having done this, write a brief justification of your placement, explaining why some of the challenges were more serious than others. The resulting diagram could form the basis of an essay plan.

How serious were the problems facing Weimar in the period from the end of the First World War to 1923?

1 The Kaiser was still popular.
2 Many Germans were shocked that Germany lost the war.
3 The new government lacked popular support.
4 The terms of the Treaty of Versailles were unpopular and the government was blamed for signing it.
5 Germany had to pay significant reparations.
6 There was much support for political parties on the left and right who did not support democracy.
7 The government struggled to deal with the unrest.
8 German territory was invaded by France and Belgium.

Least serious   Most serious

Stresemann and the Golden Years

The appointment of Gustav Stresemann and the establishment of a 'Great Coalition' in September 1923 are often seen as the beginning of a period of recovery for the Republic. Passive resistance in the Ruhr was ended and a new currency, the **Rentenmark**, was introduced.

Economic recovery

Industrial production gradually recovered, so that by 1927 it had returned to pre-First World War levels. The recovery was helped by loans of 800 million marks from America with the **Dawes Plan**, which also rescheduled reparation payments.

Stabilising the economy resulted in the cost of exports rising; therefore, industrialists looked to cut their costs, often by making workers redundant. Germany also became heavily dependent on loans, which, if withdrawn, would have a serious impact.

Agriculture did not fully recover and was then hit by a depression in 1927 due to global overproduction. Farmers complained that food was imported so that in return Germany could export industrial goods. This created resentment in the countryside.

Political stability

Coalitions continued to be unstable as the largest parties, the SPD and liberals, disagreed over economic and social policies.

Parties that supported democracy did well in these years, so that by 1928 they had 136 more seats than radical parties, with the Nazis winning less than 3 per cent of the vote. However, support for the liberal parties did decline and **special-interest parties** gained support.

In 1925 Hindenburg was elected president. His support for the Republic was lukewarm; he wanted to exclude the SPD from government and bring in the right-wing DNVP.

Social improvements

During the Stresemann years there were numerous social improvements:
- Wages for workers rose.
- An eight-hour day was introduced.
- The standard of living rose.
- Welfare benefits and pensions increased.

However, there were still problems:
- Farmworkers' earnings were only half the national average by 1929.
- There were still extremes of wealth and poverty.
- There were wage disputes and strikes.
- There was concern about the cost of the welfare system and the level of taxation.

Foreign policy success?

It appeared that Stresemann was able to achieve a number of foreign policy successes, which revised the Treaty of Versailles in Germany's favour. However, many of the agreements angered the nationalists, who did not want to negotiate with their former enemies.
- The Locarno Treaties of 1925 guaranteed Germany's frontiers with France and Belgium, but not Germany's frontiers in the east.
- In 1926, Germany joined the League of Nations.
- In January 1927, the Allied Disarmament Commission withdrew from Germany.
- In August 1927, Allied troops were withdrawn from garrisons in the Rhineland.
- The **Young Plan**, which reduced reparations, was signed in 1929, and Britain and France agreed to evacuate the Rhineland by the end of June 1930.

The flourishing of culture

Architecture flourished, seen in the works of the **Bauhaus** group. Painters, such as Otto Dix, formed the New Objectivity Movement. The film industry grew, producing controversial films, such as *All Quiet on the Western Front*, which angered nationalists. Jazz was popular in the nightclubs and bars in many cities.

Success?

Despite the achievements:
- The Republic did not win loyalty from either the left or the right.
- Many were scandalised by the culture, particularly the cabaret clubs, which mocked the values of the 'old Germany' with jazz and often nudity.
- The economy was burdened by the war, the cost of welfare and reparations.
- Governments were short-lived, as a result of unstable coalitions.

However, there were signs of recovery and stability in many cities.

Develop the detail   a

Below are a sample exam question and a paragraph written in answer to this question. The paragraph contains a limited amount of detail. Annotate the paragraph to add additional detail to the answer.

'The years 1924–29 were successful for the Weimar Republic.' How far do you agree?

Between 1924 and 1929, the Weimar government was largely successful. The government was able to bring about some economic recovery, although the recovery was not complete and depended on help from outside the country. Conditions for workers also improved and they gained many benefits. The political situation was also more stable; support for extreme parties fell and support for those that supported democracy increased. Foreign policy was also a success, although some groups were angered by the agreements. However, Stresemann did improve relations with European powers and Germany was able to join international organisations.

Using knowledge to support or contradict an argument

Below are a sample AS Level exam question with an interpretation written by a historian. You must read the quotation, identify the argument, and use your own knowledge to support and provide a counter-argument, challenging the interpretation offered.

'The Weimar Republic never really won the loyalty of the German people, and economically it was burdened by the legacy of a lost war and the heavy costs of running a welfare state.'

Adapted from: Mary Fulbrook, *Democracy and Dictatorship in Germany 1919–1963* (2008)

Evaluate the strengths and limitations of this interpretation, making reference to other interpretations that you have studied.

- What is the view of the interpretation?
- What knowledge of your own do you have that supports the interpretation?
- What knowledge of your own do you have that challenges the interpretation?

The impact of the Great Depression

In October 1929, the US stock market collapsed. The Wall Street Crash led to a world economic crisis.

Economic impact

The Great Depression had a particularly severe impact on Germany because of American loans and investment. The collapse of the American economy resulted in US firms and banks recalling the loans. The problems began in the autumn of 1928, but by spring 1929, unemployment in Germany had climbed to 2.5 million. The Wall Street Crash only added to the problem.

- Unemployment continued to rise.
- Demand for German goods collapsed.
- Loans on which Germany relied were recalled.
- Production was cut back, creating more unemployment.

▼ Table 1.1 Unemployment (millions) in Germany, 1929–33

Year	January	July
1928	1,862	1,012
1929	2,850	1,251
1930	3,218	2,765
1931	4,887	3,990
1932	6,042	5,392
1933	6,014	4,464

By 1932, nearly one-third of workers were registered unemployed, while others were working shorter hours or had taken pay cuts. This led to increased poverty and people were unable to pay rents and mortgages.

Government income fell, so the government struggled to pay benefits, as the system was designed to cope with only 800,000 unemployed.

Political impact

Many young unemployed joined paramilitary groups, such as the Nazi **SA** (*Sturmabteilung*) or the Communist **Rotfront**. This gave them a sense of belonging and something to do.

The Depression weakened the Great Coalition. Divisions over the unemployment insurance system created a crisis.

The SPD did not want cuts, while the German People's Party (DVP) argued for cuts. Industrialists argued that the **welfare state** should be abolished because of costs.

An attempt at compromise failed and the Cabinet resigned. This weakened democracy. Hindenburg used the opportunity to bring in the right-wing **Heinrich Brüning**, who supported Hindenburg's policy of rearming Germany.

Brüning did not have a majority and stated that if he was defeated he would ask for the Reichstag to be dissolved and rule by **emergency decree**. This happened following attempts to increase taxes and cut welfare. Historians have disagreed about his aims:

- Some have argued that he was worried hyperinflation would return.
- Some have argued that he wanted to provoke a crisis so reparations would be cancelled.

Elections took place in September 1930, which allowed the Nazi Party (see page 18) to make considerable gains. It appeared to offer simple solutions to Germany's problems.

Although the Nazis made considerable gains in the election, it still left a divided Reichstag and problems continued in 1931 and 1932, giving the impression to many that democracy was unable to deal with the situation, while unemployment continued to rise. Brüning had to rely increasingly on rule by emergency decree, which further weakened democracy.

As the government appeared unable to deal with the crisis, people turned more and more to extreme parties, not just the Nazis. Support for communism also grew, and this worried industrialists and the middle class.

The banking crisis of July 1931

The Austrian bank Kreditanstalt collapsed in July 1931. Banks had only a small amount of money in reserve, and with the collapse of Kreditanstalt, customers in other banks began to withdraw their money. Banks were forced to close and the government was forced to support them.

This event led to France blocking plans for an emergency loan to Germany. However, it was agreed that a one-year suspension of reparation payments should be allowed, and in 1932, a committee of international financial experts agreed that reparations and inter-Allied debts should be cancelled. However, in May 1932, Brüning was dismissed, leading to a period of further instability and a rapid change in chancellors (see page 20).

Simple essay style

Below is a sample exam question. Use your own knowledge, the information on the opposite page and information from other sections of the book to produce a plan for this question. Choose four general points, and provide three pieces of specific information to support each general point. Once you have planned your essay, write the introduction and conclusion for the essay. The introduction should list the points to be discussed in the essay and outline the argument you intend to make. The conclusion should summarise the key points and justify which point was the most important.

Assess the reasons why the Nazis gained popularity in the period 1929–33.

 Develop the detail **a**

Below are a sample exam question and a paragraph written in answer to this question. The paragraph contains a limited amount of detail. Annotate the paragraph to add additional detail to the answer.

'The most important impact of the Great Depression was the collapse of the Great Coalition.' How far do you agree?

The impact of the Great Depression in Germany was particularly severe because it led to loans being recalled and the economy needed these to survive. As a result, many people became unemployed and this had an impact on the political situation, as they lost faith in the government and looked to other parties to solve their problems. The government was weakened as the Depression created policy divisions within it. The government was also seen as weak because it could not control the country. The collapse of the government led to the appointment of a more right-wing chancellor, and his method of government suggested that democracy could not deal with the problems Germany faced, encouraging support for other parties.

The rise and appeal of the Nazis

The NSDAP (National Socialist German Workers' Party), or Nazis, had begun as the German Workers' Party, under the leadership of **Anton Drexler**. Hitler attended meetings and was soon placed in charge of **propaganda** and political ideas. In 1920, it announced its **25-point programme** and changed its name to the NSDAP. In 1921, Hitler became leader.

The Munich Putsch, 1923

Hitler's attempt to seize power in Bavaria failed (see page 12), but it had important consequences:
- It led to a change in tactics, as Hitler decided to win power through the ballot box.
- It brought him national publicity.

Following the putsch, the light sentence of five years (although he served only nine months), showed there was sympathy for his views.

The Nazi Party, 1924–9

While he was in prison, Hitler wrote the book *Mein Kampf*, which set out his ideas for Germany. During this time, the party collapsed and he had to rebuild it. There was little support for the party, as Weimar appeared to be recovering (see page 14). Although the Nazis won 32 seats in elections in 1924, this decreased to 14 by the end of the year and 12 in 1928.

Hitler also used the time to build up support. A network of local parties and the **Hitler Youth** and Students' League were established. In 1929, **Goebbels** was put in charge of propaganda.

The Depression

It was the impact of the Depression that allowed the Nazis to make an electoral breakthrough.

Year	Number of seats in the Reichstag
1928	12
1930	107
July 1932	230
November 1932	196
1933	288

There were a number of reasons why the Depression increased support for the Nazis:
- The Weimar government appeared weak and unable to deal with the crisis.
- Unemployment was rising and the Nazis offered public works to reduce it.
- Many people feared communism, and support for it was growing due to the Depression.

However, other factors also helped to increase support and enabled the Nazis to become the largest single party, even if they did not have a majority by July 1932:
- Support of industrialists – they were frightened of communism, so they turned to the Nazis and gave them financial backing.
- The Nazis made promises to various groups in society – the unemployed were promised jobs, businesses were promised restored profits, and farmers were promised higher prices for their produce.
- Propaganda – this was used to reinforce Nazi promises and to attack communism. They used radio broadcasts, posters, rallies and parades to reach all voters.
- Technology – in 1932, Hitler used a plane to fly to election meetings.
- Organisation – the party had been reorganised in the 1920s and local leaders were well trained.
- Image of Hitler – propaganda showed him as a strong leader and he was an excellent speaker.
- Opposition – this was weak and divided and did not see the Nazis as a serious threat.

Not all who voted for the Nazis shared their views, but they shared Nazi fears – this is known as negative cohesion. However, the election results for November 1932 suggest that support for the Nazis had peaked and was starting to decline.

! Mind map

Make a copy of the mind map below and use the information on the opposite page and the next page to add detail to it, showing how each issue was either a strength or a challenge for the Nazis in their attempts to gain power.

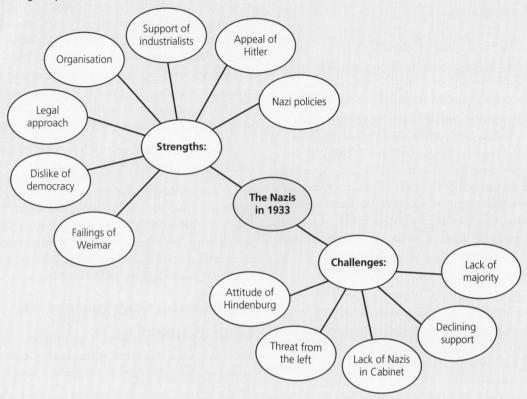

♦ RAG – rate the timeline

Below are a sample exam question and a timeline. Read the question, study the timeline and, using three coloured pens, put a red, amber or green star next to the events to show:

- Red – events and policies that have no relevance to the question
- Amber – events and policies that have some relevance to the question
- Green – events and policies that are directly relevant to the question.

To what extent was increased support for the Nazi Party in the period 1928–33 the result of rising unemployment?

1919	Start of Weimer Republic
1920	Hitler becomes leader of the Nazi Party; creation of the SA
1923	Hyperinflation and the Munich Putsch
1924	Hitler in prison, writes *Mein Kampf*
1924	Nazis win 32 seats
1929	Wall Street Crash
1929	Goebbels is put in charge of Nazi propaganda
1930–32	Chancellor Brüning's policies are unpopular
1932	Unemployment reaches 6 million
1932	Support for the Nazi Party falls in November election
1933	Hindenburg invites Hitler to be chancellor
1933	Reichstag fire; Enabling Act; banning of other political parties

Hitler's admission to power in January 1933

With the Nazi vote falling in the November 1932 election, it is perhaps surprising that Hitler was appointed chancellor in January 1933. There were a number of reasons for his appointment.

The failure of von Papen

Although the Nazis were the largest party in the Reichstag after the July 1932 election, it was **Franz von Papen** who was appointed chancellor. He wanted to create a more **authoritarian state**. He ended the ban on the SA, which led to an increase in street violence. Violence in Hamburg led to von Papen taking over the Prussian state government, as it could no longer maintain order. This destroyed the idea of each state in Germany having power over certain aspects of government, such as the police (known as the federal principle), and led to increased power being given to the national government (known as the centralisation of the state).

Hitler had demanded the right to form a government as the largest party, but was offered the post of vice chancellor, which he rejected. Von Papen did not have a majority, and with the support of the president was determined to dissolve the Reichstag and hold fresh elections. However, this failed, as the opposition passed a vote of no confidence.

New elections were held in November 1932, but the Nazis lacked the funds for a dynamic campaign. Their involvement in a transport strike in Berlin appeared to show that they were moving to the left and this frightened many middle-class voters. As a result, they lost 2 million votes.

The failure of von Schleicher

With the army unwilling to support von Papen, the government was dismissed and **Kurt von Schleicher** was appointed chancellor on 2 December 1932. He approached some Nazis to join the government, but Hitler blocked it. He also tried to get the support of the SPD and trade unions through promising economic reforms. This worried industrialists, who now looked to a von Papen–Hitler coalition.

'Backstairs intrigue'

This is the term used by the historian Alan Bullock to describe how Hitler came to power. Having been removed from power, von Papen began talks with Hitler, using intermediaries. With von Schleicher unable to gain a majority in the Reichstag, Hitler's position was strengthened. Hindenburg lost confidence in von Schleicher and instructed von Papen to talk with Hitler. Hindenburg and his advisers believed that the Nazis were in decline and therefore would be easier to control.

Hindenburg withdrew support from von Schleicher, who resigned on 28 January 1933.

Hitler demanded the position of chancellor and the positions of minister of the interior and minister for Prussia for other Nazis. Von Papen agreed, as nationalists would be in nine other positions in the Cabinet. On 28 January, Hindenburg agreed. Hitler was appointed chancellor on 30 January 1933.

Could Hitler's appointment have been avoided?

Some have argued that Hitler's popularity depended on unemployment, and that once unemployment fell, so would support for the Nazis. By December 1932:
- The Nazi Party was nearly bankrupt.
- The economy was starting to recover.
- Unable to gain power, the Nazis' promises could not be fulfilled.

However, Hitler's appointment became more likely as Hindenburg and von Papen had been unable to establish an authoritarian government. In order to get into power, von Papen had no choice but to form a coalition with Hitler. It appeared that with the Nazis having only three seats in the Cabinet, their power would be limited and could soon be dispensed with.

Support or challenge?
a

Below is an exam-style question which asks you how far you agree with a specific statement. Below this are a series of general statements that are relevant to the question. Using your own knowledge and the information on the opposite page, decide which general statements support or challenge the statement in the question and tick the appropriate box in each case.

'Hitler and the Nazi Party seized power in January 1933.' How far do you agree with this statement?

	Support	Challenge
Hitler's appointment as chancellor was the result of constitutional procedures.		
Nazi support was in decline and therefore they had to seize power.		
It was electoral support that brought Hitler to power.		
Intrigue, rather than seizure of power, best describes Hitler's appointment as chancellor.		
Rather than the Nazis seizing power, other figures believed they were using Hitler.		
Hitler came to power only because Hindenburg and von Papen had been unable to establish an authoritarian government.		
Hitler came to power because he demanded that he was appointed chancellor because the Nazis were the largest party.		
Hitler's dislike of democracy resulted in the events of January 1933 being called a seizure of power.		
Hitler and the Nazi Party came to power because of their electoral strength.		

Recommended reading

As this is an area of great historical debate and is part of the topics that could be set for the AS Level interpretation question, it is worth spending some time studying it in some depth, as it will enhance your understanding of the debates. Below is a list of suggested further reading on this topic.

● Alan Bullock, *Hitler: A Study in Tyranny* (1990)
● Richard Evans, *The Coming of the Third Reich* (2004)
● John Hiden, *Longman Seminar Studies in History: The Weimar Republic*, pages 1–71 (1996)
● Geoff Layton, *Access to History: Democracy and Dictatorships in Germany 1919–63*, Chapters 1–3 (2015)
● Geoff Layton, *Access to History: From Bismarck to Hitler: Germany 1890–1933*, pages 73–144 (1999)

Exam focus

Below are a sample exam question and a model answer. Read the question, and then the answer and the comments around it.

Assess the reasons for Hitler coming to power in January 1933.

Without the onset of the Depression, it is arguable that the Nazis would have remained a minority party of the extreme right, with little chance of major electoral success. In the elections of 1924 and 1928, the Nazis won 14 and 12 seats respectively in the Reichstag. However, as the Depression began to bite, Nazi electoral fortunes were transformed, the NSDAP winning 107 seats in 1930 and 230 in July 1932, becoming the largest party in the Reichstag. The economic and social effects of the Depression, with a 60 per cent drop in foreign trade and 6 million unemployed, undermined the relative political stability that Germany had achieved in the later 1920s. Faith in the ability of Weimar democracy, never strong, was fatally fractured as co-operation between democratic parties broke down over what to do about the Depression. The Great Coalition broke up in 1930, and no lasting government was able to replace it or deal with the severe problems the Depression produced. As problems mounted and democratic parties squabbled, people began to turn to alternatives – the communist recipe proved attractive to many workers, while the extreme nationalism and vague promises of the Nazis won support on the right.

The Depression brought to the fore the weaknesses that the Weimar system of government had had from the start. Democracy, a condition of peace at the end of the war, was from the start associated with the defeat and humiliation of Germany and the signing of the hated Treaty of Versailles. Germans were not used to democracy, and while there were established political parties like the Social Democrats and the Centre Party, the new system, with election by proportional representation, allowed new and extreme parties like the Nazis and the communists to gain representation and made it impossible for a government to be formed without a coalition. The instability of the Weimar system is reflected in the fact that the average lifespan of a Weimar government was just eight months.

The Depression and the weaknesses of the Weimar Republic provided the necessary conditions for the rise of political extremism in Germany. However, these factors alone do not explain the rise to power of Hitler. After all, the only party to increase its proportion of the vote consistently in the four elections between 1928 and 1932 was not the Nazi Party, whose proportion of the vote fell in November 1932, but the Communist Party. The rise in support for the Nazi Party had much to do with Hitler, Nazi Party organisation and the programme and propaganda it put forward.

There is no doubt about the personal impact Hitler made. The impact of his speech-making is well documented. He had the ability to tap into people's hopes and fears and play on their emotions, tailoring his speeches, as Goebbels tailored Nazi propaganda, to his audience. To the unemployed he promised work and bread; to big business and the middle classes he promised the destruction of communism; he praised farmers as the backbone of the nation; to all he promised a German revival, strong government and the overturning of Versailles.

Offers a view, although not directly as to a possible main reason.

Detailed support is given for the reason why the Depression was important.

The importance of the Depression is further explained.

The opening sentence links the Depression to the weakness of the Weimar system – links between factors help to take answers into the higher levels.

The paragraph goes on to develop and explain the weaknesses of the Weimar system, with detailed support.

The opening sentence links another factor to the Depression – the rise of political extremism.

Precise evidence as to how Hitler tailored his speeches is given, and the answer does not simply rely on generalisations about his oratory skills.

For all, he provided scapegoats for Germany's problems in the Jews, the communists and democratic politicians. Anti-communism was a powerful weapon in Hitler's electoral success. Words and deeds, such as street fighting and the disruption of meetings, convinced many that he was the only one who could prevent a possible communist revolution. Hitler was also a shrewd political operator, charming industrialists and winning support from media moguls like Alfred Hugenberg.

By 1928, the Nazi Party was a well-organised national party, with over 100,000 members. It had its own private army, the SA, to provide the disciplined, uniformed, flag-bearing men for publicity marches and to take the fight to rival parties and communists. It had a propaganda genius in Goebbels, whose carefully orchestrated campaigns did much to keep Hitler and the Nazis in the limelight, and to project an image of determination, action and hope that appealed to a nation disillusioned with democracy and facing economic and social despair.

And yet, what finally brought Hitler to power was not success with the electorate, but the intrigues at the top of the political system. Winning the election in July 1932 did not bring him the chancellorship; a decline in electoral support in the election of November seemed to suggest the Nazi bolt was shot. However, it was at this point that Hitler was to achieve political power. The political rivalry between von Schleicher and von Papen, and the 'backstairs intrigue' during the winter of 1932–33, resulted in von Papen convincing the aged President Hindenburg (who, although a nationalist and no lover of democracy, hated Hitler) that Hitler should be made chancellor in a coalition government. Von Papen's miscalculation that he could control Hitler was fateful.

A combination of factors, then, explains Hitler's coming to power. The impact of defeat and humiliation in the First World War, the weaknesses of the Weimar Republic and the impact of the Depression provided necessary conditions for the rise in Nazi support. Hitler's abilities and leadership, and Nazi Party organisation and propaganda enabled Hitler to exploit the situation, but the immediate cause was the political judgements by von Papen and Hindenburg, which led to Hitler's appointment as chancellor in January 1933.

Once again, the answer has precise evidence, in the form of the media mogul and nationalist Hugenberg.

A large number of points are raised in the paragraph, but each has some support. The answer uses the information to take the argument forward and does not simply describe developments.

This is a confusing period, but the answer explains the intrigue and how it helped bring Hitler to power; the chronology is accurate.

The answer explains that it is a combination of reasons rather than just one 'most important' factor and this approach is fine, provided it has been shown in the rest of the essay – which was the case through a series of links.

This is a clearly argued and well-focused response. The answer explains the importance of a range of factors and supports the argument with precise, accurate and relevant knowledge. There is evidence of linkage between factors and this is supported in the judgement, suggesting that the argument is logically developed. As a result, it would be placed in the higher levels.

Reverse engineering

Although the answer scored well, the answer lacks an opening paragraph that outlines the argument and the view of the candidate about the issue in the question. Write an opening paragraph that introduces the line of argument to be pursued and the issues to be discussed.

Exam focus

Below are a sample exam question for the AS Level interpretation question and a model answer. Read the question, and then the answer and the comments around it.

'Germany's economic recovery [in the period to 1929] was built on poor foundations that created a false idea of prosperity.'

Geoff Layton, *Democracy and Dictatorships 1919–63* (2015)

Evaluate the strengths and limitations of this interpretation, making reference to other interpretations that you have studied.

The interpretation is suggesting that the recovery of the German economy, after the problems caused by the war and the difficulties of 1919–23, particularly the hyperinflation and the problem of reparations, was never very secure. It argues that although there appeared to be some signs of prosperity in the period – hence its name, the 'Golden Years' – it was not built on solid foundations. However, some have seen these years as the high point of the Weimar Republic, and argued that they were stable and that it was only events that were outside the control of Weimar that brought about its subsequent collapse, claiming that economic, as well as political stability were returning to Germany.

It is true that to some extent Germany's economic recovery was built on poor foundations. It was heavily reliant on loans, particularly from the USA, to fund its recovery, and therefore the prosperity was reliant on credit from abroad. It would therefore be correct to argue that the German economic recovery depended on international forces and pressures over which it had no real control, so that when the Depression and Wall Street Crash hit the USA, Germany suffered more than most nations. Moreover, investors had been badly hit by the inflation of 1923 and were therefore less willing to invest, making the recovery even more dependent on foreign loans and too weak to encourage growth. Although production levels did recover to pre-war levels by 1928, the interpretation is correct in that the recovery was based on weak foundations, as world economic conditions did not favour Germany: protective tariffs limited exports, and they were further hit by the loss of resource-rich lands, such as Alsace-Lorraine, as a result of the Treaty of Versailles. There was certainly a false sense of prosperity, which even the government appeared to have succumbed to as they spent large sums on the welfare state, suggesting that they believed the economy was in a better position than was actually the case. The problems facing the German economy are even more evident and support the view in the interpretation if farming is taken into account, as grain production did not return to its pre-war levels and many farmers were in debt; with incomes 44 per cent below the national average, they were not prospering. Poor foundations can also be seen by looking at unemployment rates, which never fell below 1.3 million and were even higher before the Crash and the withdrawal of loans.

The response begins by explaining the interpretation; this is crucial, allowing the candidate, having unpicked the given interpretation, to examine its strengths and limitations.

The answer is able to place the given interpretation in the wider historical debate about the success of Weimar in the period that has been called the 'Golden Years'.

Relevant and accurate own knowledge is directly linked to the given interpretation to show the strengths of the interpretation.

There is further detailed own knowledge linked to the interpretation to further explain its strengths.

Further precise evidence is used to evaluate the interpretation.

The theme of detailed knowledge being applied to the interpretation is evident throughout the paragraph.

However, the interpretation does ignore the considerable recovery that had been made. Production levels, by 1928, had surpassed those prior to the First World War, suggesting that without the Crash they would have continued to grow. The interpretation also ignores the considerable resources that Germany did possess, and its ability to improve efficiency and methods of production, particularly in the coal and steel industries. The interpretation suggests that the foundations were poor, yet exports rose by some 40 per cent between 1925 and 1929. The interpretation also ignores other advantages that German industry possessed, such as being able to lower costs because of cartels, which had better purchasing power than smaller industries, allowing German manufacturing, particularly chemical, to grow.

The answer makes it very clear that there are limitations to the interpretation.

A good range of own knowledge is applied and directly linked to the interpretation to illustrate its weaknesses.

The answer explains the interpretation and places it in the wider context of the debate about the extent of the recovery of Weimar in this period and whether it should be seen as the 'Golden Years'. Detailed knowledge is directly applied to the interpretation to show both its strengths and limitations, and throughout the focus remains on evaluating the given interpretation, not other interpretations.

Reverse engineering

Answers to interpretation questions should start by placing the given interpretation in the wider context of the historical debate about the issue. This interpretation is about the economic recovery of Weimar in the years 1924–29. The last sentence of the opening paragraph refers to the debate over political stability. Rewrite the opening paragraph for an interpretation that argues that political stability was built on weak foundations and created a false sense of stability.

2 The establishment of the Nazi dictatorship and its domestic policies, February 1933 to 1939

Hitler's consolidation of power

Although Hitler had been appointed chancellor, his power was far from absolute. But over the next 18 months, he transformed his position into that of a **totalitarian** dictator.

The legal revolution

Hitler created a dictatorship using legal methods.

27 February 1933: Reichstag fire

The parliament building in Berlin was burnt down and the communists were blamed and banned. The fire was used to justify measures against the communists.

28 February 1933: Decree for the Protection of the People and the State

As a result of the fire, Hitler was granted emergency powers. Political and civil liberties were suspended and many anti-Nazis were arrested.

5 March 1933: Election

Hitler called fresh elections to the Reichstag in the hope of winning an overall majority. The Nazi vote increased to 43.9 per cent. Nationalist support was still needed.

23 March 1933: Enabling Act

With many members absent and others intimidated, the Reichstag voted for the **Enabling Act** by the necessary two-thirds majority to give Hitler total power and therefore end democracy. Parliamentary procedure and legislation came to an end. Full power was transferred to the chancellor and government. A dictatorship based on legality was created.

14 July 1933: The Nazi Party became the only legal party

Hitler used his powers to ban other political parties. Germany became a one-party state.

Co-ordination (*Gleichschaltung*)

Gleichschaltung was the Nazification of society, ensuring co-operation with the regime. It was put into practice at a local level – 'revolution from below' – by the SA, and at a national level – 'revolution from above' – from Berlin.

The idea was to merge German society with Nazi Party institutions and associations, with the aim of allowing Nazis to control cultural, social and educational activity. However, the first concern was political, as Table 2.1 shows.

▼ Table 2.1 The co-ordination of German institutions

Institution	What happened?
Federal states	Regional parliaments were dissolved and then abolished
	Reich governors were created
	Federal government and governors were subordinated to central government
Political parties	Communists were banned after the Reichstag fire
	The Social Democratic Party was banned and its assets seized
	Most parties agreed to dissolve themselves
	The Nazis became the only legal party
Trade unions	Union premises were occupied, funds were seized and leaders were sent to concentration camps
	Independent unions were banned and replaced by the German Labour Front (DAF)

Success?

In some areas, the Nazis did have control. However, they did not control the Church, army or big business, and had only partial control of the civil service and education. Hitler's power was limited because he did not want to lose the support of important groups. However, he was under pressure from the SA to implement further changes.

The Night of the Long Knives

Hitler had to deal with opposition within his own party. SA chief **Ernst Röhm** wanted to merge the army and the SA. Army chiefs refused, due to the SA's indiscipline. Hitler chose to execute Röhm and the SA leaders on the 'Night of the Long Knives' in June 1934. This had many consequences:

- It removed the SA and won the support of the conservative right. The army took an oath of personal loyalty to Hitler.
- The **SS** (*Schutzstaffel* – Hitler's personal guard), which had been a wing of the SA, emerged as an independent organisation.
- Hitler secured his dictatorship: he had been allowed to get away with the legal murder of opponents.

Hitler's dominance was confirmed when Hindenburg died in August 1934 and Hitler merged the roles of chancellor and president into that of Führer.

ℹ️ Introducing an argument

Below are a sample exam question, a list of key points to be made in the essay, and a simple introduction and conclusion for the essay. Read these and then, using the information on the opposite page and pages 28, 30, 32 and 36, rewrite the introduction and the conclusion in order to develop an argument.

'Hitler was able to establish complete control over all aspects of German life.' How far do you agree?

Key points:
- Other political parties, such as the SPD and the communists
- Trade unions
- Churches
- Big business
- The army
- The SA

Introduction:

To an extent, Hitler was able to establish complete control over all aspects of German life, as all political parties and trade unions were abolished, which meant the Nazis were the only party. However, in some areas, such as the Church, the army and business, he did not establish complete control.

Conclusion:

To some extent, the Nazis had been able to establish complete control. Nazi policies had removed much opposition and made Germany a single-party state. However, there were groups and institutions that the Nazi Party did not control in this period.

⭐ RAG – rate the timeline

Below are a sample exam question and a timeline. Read the question, study the timeline and, using three coloured pens, put a red, amber or green star next to the events to show:

- Red – events and policies that have no relevance to the question
- Amber – events and policies that have some relevance to the question
- Green – events and policies that are directly relevant to the question.

'The most important event in Hitler establishing a dictatorship was the Reichstag fire.' How far do you agree?

1924	Hitler decides to achieve power by legal methods
1929	Himmler appointed head of the SS
July 1932	Nazis are the largest party in the election
November 1932	Support for Nazis falls in the election
January 1933	Hitler is appointed chancellor
February 1933	Reichstag fire
March 1933	Nazis fail to win an overall majority in the election
March 1933	Enabling Act
July 1933	Other political parties are banned
June 1934	Night of the Long Knives
August 1934	Death of Hindenburg

Now repeat the activity with the following questions:

To what extent was Hitler an all-powerful dictator by the end of 1933?

'Support for the Nazis was the most important reason Hitler was able to establish a dictatorship.' How far do you agree?

2 The establishment of the Nazi dictatorship and its domestic policies, February 1933 to 1939

OCR AS and A-Level Democracy and Dictatorships in Germany 1919–1963

27

Hitler and the system of government and administration

What was Hitler's role?

The image of the Führer was of an all-powerful dictator. He was leader of the party and combined the roles of chancellor, president and commander-in-chief of the armed forces. His will was law, both in the party and in Germany, at least in theory. He was portrayed as having the vision and will to transform Germany.

However, although Hitler had destroyed much of the opposition, there were still rival power systems which overlapped. These included the central government, with the ministries and civil service, and the SS and the Nazi Party.

As a result Hitler's role was limited:
- There was no all-embracing constitution in the Third Reich. This meant that government and law emerged in a haphazard form.
- In practice, no individual could control all areas of government.
- Hitler relied on subordinates to put his wishes into practice.
- Hitler's own personality and lifestyle involved long sleeping hours and absences from Berlin.

Hitler's day-to-day role was limited. He avoided decision-making and had little contact with ministers, who had to determine his wishes. This was known as 'working towards the Führer' and often resulted in contradictions. Hitler disliked paperwork and committees, and did not co-ordinate government. The role of the Cabinet declined – it met 72 times in 1933, but only four times in 1936. The last formal meeting was in 1938. This lack of clear leadership often resulted in chaos.

War in 1939 added to the problems. Hitler was away at the front, but would not allow Cabinet meetings or give committees power, as he feared they might challenge him. Decisions were only made by seeing Hitler, and **Martin Bormann** controlled this. Hitler rarely made decisions outside of foreign policy, but dominated government through his charisma.

What was the role of the Nazi Party and the state?

In theory, Germany was a one-party, totalitarian state, reinforced by propaganda. However, in practice, this was not true; there were limits to the power of the Nazi Party:
- It never destroyed established state institutions.
- Party divisions remained.

As the bureaucracy of the state was already established and effective, Hitler did not destroy the old institutions, such as the ministries, run by civil servants who were often conservative, or the **judiciary**, and he never clarified their relationship to the Nazi Party. This led to conflict, overlap and confusion, and created **dualism**, where the forces of the Nazi Party, such as the Hitler Youth, SS and *Gauleiters*, and the German state co-existed as rival centres of power.

There were attempts to improve party influence after 1938. Rudolf Hess, as deputy Führer, insisted that civil servants had to be party members and increased party supervision. Bormann created the Department for Internal Party Affairs to discipline the party structure, and the Department for Affairs of State to secure party supremacy over the state.

⚠ Delete as applicable

Below are a sample exam question and a paragraph written in answer to this question. Read the paragraph and decide which of the options (in bold) is the most appropriate. Delete the least appropriate options and complete the paragraph by justifying your selection.

'Hitler was only ever a weak dictator.' How far do you agree?

> Hitler was to a **limited/fair/great** extent only ever a weak dictator. This is because he **always/sometimes/ never** relied on subordinates to put his will into practice, as he was **always/sometimes/never** interested in the day-to-day running of the government. This situation was reinforced as Hitler **always/sometimes/never** had contact with ministers and therefore they followed the policy of 'working towards the Führer'. War ensured that these issues **grew/remained the same/declined** as Hitler **allowed/did not allow** the Cabinet to meet. However, Hitler **always/sometimes/never** made decisions about foreign policy.
>
> _____
>
> _____

⦿ Identify an argument

Below are a series of definitions, a sample exam question and two sample paragraphs. One of the paragraphs achieves a high level because it contains an argument and a judgement. The other achieves a lower level because it contains only description and assertion. Using the information from earlier in the book and the opposite page, identify which is which. The mark schemes on page 7 will help you.

- **Description**: a detailed account
- **Assertion**: an opinion that is not supported by a fact or reason
- **Reason**: a statement which explains or justifies something
- **Argument**: an assertion justified with a reason
- **Judgement**: an assertion that is supported by a fact or reason

To what extent was Hitler's role in government limited?

Answer 1:

> Hitler was the Führer and held the offices of chancellor, president and commander-in-chief of the armed forces. His will was law in the party and in Germany. The role of the Cabinet declined; it met on fewer occasions as the period progressed, with the last formal meeting in 1938. During the war, Hitler was at the front and did not allow the Cabinet to meet and did not give committees power to make decisions. For much of the time he slept long hours and was not in Berlin. Hitler made decisions about foreign policy.

Answer 2:

> In theory, Hitler was an all-powerful dictator, with his will the law, but there were a number of issues that limited his role in government. Even had Hitler wanted to, it would have been difficult to control all areas of government, but given his lifestyle of long hours of sleep and frequent absences from Berlin, subordinates had to put his wishes into practice. Moreover, as Hitler often avoided decision-making, they had to try to determine his wishes in a policy known as 'working towards the Führer'. As a result there was a lack of clear leadership and this was even worse during the war.

Censorship and propaganda

The Nazis relied on several methods to maintain control. Propaganda was used to win over the public and help create a *Volksgemeinschaft* through:

● glorifying war and the **Aryan** race
● spreading Nazism and Nazi values.

It was also used in wartime in order to mobilise people, sustain morale and provide practical advice on air raids, recycling food and 'careless talk'.

Responsibility for propaganda was given to **Goebbels**, who was made minister of public enlightenment and propaganda. Departments were established to run the press, film, radio and theatre. They censored all non-Nazi culture and media and promoted Nazi **ideology**.

Nazi ideology

The main beliefs of the Nazi Party involved:

● the maintenance of racial purity
● a hierarchy of races, with Aryans at the top and Jews and Slavs at the bottom
● blaming the Jews for all of Germany's problems
● anti-democratic – Germany needed a strong dictatorship, a one-party state
● nationalism – the Treaty of Versailles had to be reversed and Germany needed 'living space' in the east
● a people's community that overcame class differences, was socially united and racially pure.

Some Nazis were also anti-capitalist and wanted profit-sharing.

Historians have usually assumed that Nazi propaganda was very successful, but recent work based on local studies has shown that the degree of success varied according to the purpose. It did help to create the **Hitler myth** and strengthen Germany, but was less successful in creating a Nazi culture and winning over the working classes.

Examples of propaganda

Radio

Goebbels brought broadcasting under Nazi control and created the Reich Radio Company. As only 25 per cent of Germans owned radios, the government produced cheap sets – the People's Receiver. By 1939, 70 per cent of the population had radios.

There was no escaping the Nazi message, as loudspeakers were installed in factories, cafes and offices. 'Radio wardens' co-ordinated listening. However, Goebbels was aware that too much political propaganda bored people; therefore, two-thirds of airtime was popular songs and music.

Mass communication was directly under the regime's control.

Press

Germany had a tradition of independent newspapers. Goebbels closed down socialist and communist ones and placed others under the control of the Reich Press Chamber. The Editor's Law of 1933 ensured that papers reported Nazi views, and editors were punished if they went against this. A daily press conference at the Propaganda Ministry gave editors guidance on what to write. News agencies were also placed under state control to ensure they put forward a pro-Nazi view.

Drama and music

The Nazis wanted drama and music to uphold Nazi values and therefore they exercised strict control over them. Theatres and plays had to have a licence and were subject to police supervision. They banned experimental plays and music. In music, even some classics were censored; jazz was forbidden, as it was 'degenerate'; and music by Jews was forbidden, while Jewish conductors and musicians were dismissed.

Literature and art

Writers had to be positive about Nazism. There were approved themes, such as the early days of Nazism, war and expansion. The Reich Chamber of Literature listed banned books, and libraries and second-hand bookshops were raided and banned books burned at rallies. Modernist art was banned and modern paintings were removed from galleries. Acceptable art portrayed the German countryside and heroic German warriors.

Film

The Reich Film Chamber was established and everyone in the film industry had to join. There were few political films, but the Weekly Review contained political information and had to be included in all film programmes.

Ritual

Rituals were used to unite society, strengthen the regime, win popularity and glorify the Nazi past. The regime created new social rituals, such as the *Heil Hitler* greeting. Other examples included:

● the **Horst Wessel** anthem
● uniforms
● public festivals to commemorate the seizure of power, the party's foundation, Hitler's birthday and the Munich Putsch.

Quick quizzes at **www.hoddereducation.co.uk/myrevisionnotes**

Mind map

Make a copy of the mind map below and use the information on the opposite page to add detail to it, showing how the Nazis used propaganda to increase their control over Germany.

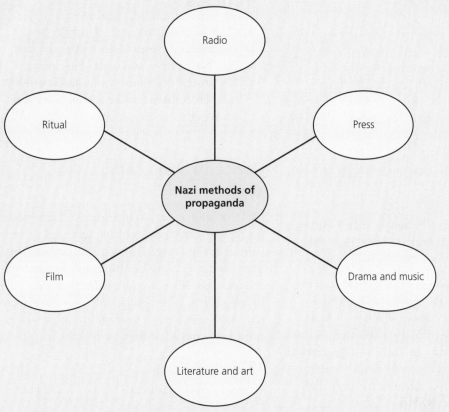

(i) **Turning assertion into argument**   a

Below are a sample question and a series of assertions. Read the exam question and then add a justification to each of the assertions to turn each one into an argument.

'Propaganda had a significant role in gaining the Nazi Party popular support.' How far do you agree?

Propaganda played a significant role in gaining the Nazi Party popular support because

_____

_____

However, the success of propaganda depended on its purpose as

_____

_____

Yet it did do much to strengthen the Hitler myth because

_____

_____

2 The establishment of the Nazi dictatorship and its domestic policies, February 1933 to 1939

The police state and terror

The Nazi regime survived largely because it was able to remove its enemies and terrorise its opponents. This was achieved through the creation of a police state consisting of a variety of groups.

The courts

- Judges were instructed to issue harsher sentences.
- There were new laws regarding political offences.
- People's courts were established to try enemies of the state.
- From 1939, judges had to study Nazi beliefs. Judges who did not carry out government wishes were removed.
- Nazis replaced senior officials.
- The SS group leader was appointed minister of justice.

The SS

Originally established as an elite bodyguard for Hitler in 1925, the SS became a 'state within a state', responsible only to Hitler. It came to dominate the police state.

In 1929, **Heinrich Himmler** became its head, and in 1931, he created the **SD** – the secret intelligence wing of the SS. In 1934, he took control of police, including the **Gestapo** in Prussia. In 1935, the SS became an elite force that only Aryans could join. In 1936, all police and Gestapo powers were placed under Himmler's control. Finally, in 1939, all party and state police organisations were amalgamated into the **RSHA**.

The SS was the key organisation in terror. It preserved the Nazi regime and became a key power group. It was made up of the SD, the Gestapo, the **Kripo** and the **Waffen SS**. Its roles included policing, intelligence gathering and, later, military functions. It was responsible for security, ideology and race, the economy and a variety of military issues.

The SS was responsible for the creation of the **'New Order'**. Himmler became 'commissioner for consolidating German nationhood', which gave him responsibility for the resettling of **ethnic Germans** from conquered territories and the elimination of groups such as Jews and gypsies.

The Gestapo

The Gestapo was the secret state police. Its role was to find opponents of the Nazis and arrest them. People arrested could be sent to concentration camps without trial. The Gestapo was a small organisation, with 20,000–40,000 agents, many of whom were little more than office workers who relied on informers and block wardens for information. Wardens were responsible for 50 houses or apartments, and ensured that Nazi flags were displayed and rallies were attended. There were about 2 million block wardens in Germany. They were unpopular in working-class areas, where there was sympathy for communists and socialists.

The impact of war on the police state

- The role of policing and security expanded.
- The military increased from three divisions to 35.
- The 'New Order' was created in occupied lands.
- The process of exterminating and resettling individuals based on race and ideology was developed.

Concentration camps

1933

Concentration camps were prisons where opponents of the regime were questioned and subjected to torture, hard labour and re-education in Nazi ideals. They were established as part of a campaign against communists and socialists. Many were closed as they were offensive to nationalists. When Himmler took control there were only 3,000 inmates, suggesting that the campaign to silence opponents had been successful.

1936

Camps focused on **asocials**, criminals and homosexuals.

1937

Any individuals who did not fit into the *Volksgemeinschaft* were imprisoned, including beggars, gypsies and the long-term unemployed.

1942

Regular prisoners and foreign workers were transferred to camps as a source of labour. The camps subsequently became extermination camps for Jews.

The numbers held within camps expanded during the war:
- September 1939: 25,000
- December 1942: 88,000
- January 1945: 714,211.

Develop the detail a

Below are a sample exam question and a paragraph written in answer to this question. The paragraph contains a limited amount of detail. Annotate the paragraph to add additional detail to the answer.

> How successful was the police state in enforcing its will on opponents of the Nazis?

> The Nazi state had a variety of groups with which to enforce its will on the people of Germany. The courts played a crucial role in this and could usually be relied on to implement Nazi wishes because of the reforms that had been made to them. The SS probably played the most important role in the organisation of terror, with its range of activities. It had a number of roles and gained influence when the Second World War broke out. It ran the concentration camps and the Nazis used these to attack political opponents and those who did not fit their ideal, with the numbers in the camps growing dramatically. Although the Gestapo was feared by many Germans, it was actually small; it was the block wardens who were the important element in imposing Nazi will at a local level.

Simple essay style

Below is a sample exam question. Use your own knowledge, the information on the opposite page and information from other sections of the book to produce a plan for this question. Choose four general points, and provide three pieces of specific information to support each general point. Once you have planned your essay, write the introduction and conclusion for the essay. The introduction should list the points to be discussed in the essay and outline the line of argument you intend to take. The conclusion should summarise the key points and justify which point was the most important.

> 'The Gestapo did more than any other organisation to enforce the police state.' How far do you agree?

2 The establishment of the Nazi dictatorship and its domestic policies, February 1933 to 1939

Opposition and resistance

Although the regime collapsed only under the pressure of military defeat and was determined to crush any opposition, many resisted. This resistance took a variety of forms:

- private grumbling to family or friends or at work
- underground resistance and open opposition to the government
- attempts to overthrow the regime and remove Hitler.

The opposition

Group	Aims and actions	Impact
Communists (most support in industrial cities)	They had cells in large cities. They produced pamphlets attacking the Nazis. Most important was the Red Orchestra, a spy network that sent information to Moscow.	Minimal, as many had been arrested after the Reichstag fire. They were more concerned with self-preservation.
Social Democrats (support in industrial areas among working class)	Banned as a political party, but retained some underground activity. Their leadership was often arrested. Produced anti-Nazi propaganda and kept the socialist message alive.	Minimal, as their greater concern was self-preservation.
Trade unions (support among factory workers)	They were weakened by arrests after 1933–34, but carried out strikes in 1935–36 and 1945.	Industrial action proved ineffective.
Churches (priests and pastors individually and as a group)	Bishop Galen of Münster attacked the policy of **euthanasia**. Most adopted a pragmatic response and preserved religious practices.	They did not provide effective opposition, although they were able to stop euthanasia temporarily. Many Church leaders were sent to camps.
Youth (those who did not enjoy the activities of the Hitler Youth or resented the loss of freedom)	Groups such as the Swing Youth, Edelweiss Pirates, Roving Dudes and Navajos often just behaved in anti-Nazi ways, such as playing dance and jazz music. They disliked the military emphasis of the Hitler Youth.	Some did attack military targets and assassinate Gestapo officers, but these activities were limited.
Students	White Rose, a student group in Munich, issued pamphlets condemning the values of the Nazi regime.	Minimal impact – leaders of White Rose were arrested and tortured.
Conservatives (often members of the civil service from the Weimar period)	The Kreisau Circle included officers, aristocrats, academics and churchmen. They drew up plans for post-Nazi Germany.	Some pacifists in the circle were opposed to a coup. Resistance only developed late on, and it was difficult to organise and plan as they feared arrest.
Army (commanders and high-ranking officers who resented Hitler's background)	There was slow development due to the Army Oath (see page 26) and early military success. However, army support of Hitler declined after defeat at Stalingrad and opposition developed. Some commanders began to plot, and this culminated in the **bomb plot** under Stauffenberg.	The bomb plot failed and officers were slow to act, allowing Hitler to regain control. About 5,000 members of the resistance were killed afterwards.

Why was there so little open opposition?

- The Nazi **'economic miracle'**: life had improved and many now had jobs and were willing to accept some of the unpopular policies.
- Terror: people were frightened of the Gestapo and concentration camps.
- Opposition groups were divided: communists and the SPD opposed each other.
- The Nazis abandoned and hid some unpopular policies: for example, criticism after **Kristallnacht** resulted in anti-Jewish measures being performed in secret.

! Support or challenge? a

Below is an exam-style question which asks you how far you agree with a specific statement. Below this are a series of general statements that are relevant to the question. Using your own knowledge and the information on the opposite page and the previous page, decide which general statements support or challenge the statement in the question and tick the appropriate box in each case.

'Opposition to the Nazi regime was limited in its appeal and effectiveness.' How far do you agree?

	Support	Challenge
Gestapo numbers were limited and this made opposition much easier.		
Opposition lacked organisation and this made it weak.		
Most people simply accepted the regime and were happy they had work.		
Opposition groups continued to exist throughout the period.		
Pamphlets that opposition groups produced had little impact.		
People were too frightened to listen to messages of opposition.		
There were a large number of different opposition groups.		
The left wing provided the most effective opposition to the Nazis.		
Defeats in the war increased opposition to the regime.		

i Developing an argument a

Below are a sample exam question, a list of key points to be made in the essay, and a paragraph from the essay. Read the question, the key points and the sample paragraph. Using the information from the opposite page and from page 36 rewrite the paragraph in order to develop an argument. Your paragraph should explain why the factor discussed in the paragraph is either the most significant factor or less significant than another factor.

'The Churches were the strongest opponents of the Nazi regime.' How far do you agree?

Key points:

- Opposition from the military developed following defeats.
- Political parties had been banned.
- Much opposition was just the production of pamphlets.
- The Churches had much support and were able to stop unpopular policies.
- Youth opposition often just listened to music.

The Churches opposed some of the Nazi policies. Bishop Galen of Münster opposed the policy of euthanasia and was able to force the government to abandon the policy temporarily. Other Church leaders, such as Bonhoeffer, were sent to concentration camps because of their opposition. There was also opposition from youth groups and students. Youth groups, such as the Edelweiss Pirates and the Swing Youth, opposed the Nazis by playing jazz music, while student groups such as the White Rose produced pamphlets attacking the Nazis. As the war progressed, some of the army began to oppose Hitler. The opposition had been slow to develop because of the early military success, but after defeat at Stalingrad it developed and culminated in the Stauffenberg plot, which attempted to kill Hitler. Political parties had been banned and largely destroyed by 1934, but they did go underground and produce pamphlets attacking the regime. However, their main concern was simply to survive.

Nazi religious policies and attitude to the Churches REVISED

The rise of Nazism was a direct challenge to Christian values, but the Churches were powerful and therefore the relationship between the two would be a challenge for the Nazi Party.

Christianity and Nazism

Christianity was a major problem for the Nazis. Christianity's teachings directly contradicted the Nazi philosophy of violence, strength and war. Moreover, Jesus was Jewish rather than Aryan, and this went against Nazi *völkisch* beliefs. This was problematic because most Germans were Christians, and those with strong religious beliefs were less likely to 'worship' Hitler.

The Protestant Church

Nonetheless, many Christians, especially in the Protestant Church, supported the Nazis because they agreed over family values. Many pastors had spoken in support of the Nazis, encouraging congregations to vote for them, and allowed their churches to be used as Nazi bases.

Co-ordinating the Protestant Church

Hitler wanted to reorganise the Protestant Church as one united Reich Church, to make it easier to control, but these plans were resisted. The Nazis appointed Otto Müller, a fanatical Nazi, as Reich bishop.

Opposition within the Protestant Church

There was some conflict between the Nazis and the Protestant Church. In 1934, two Protestant bishops were arrested for opposing the Reich Church. Pastors then set up the Confessional Church, which was independent of the state. **Pastor Martin Niemöller** led it, with the support of 7,000 out of 17,000 pastors.

The Catholic Church

The Catholic Church was concerned to preserve its independence and signed the **Concordat** in July 1933. This guaranteed religious freedom, as the Church could run itself and appoint clergy. Parents could request faith schools for their children. The Nazis also agreed not to interfere with the legal and property rights of the Church. In return, the Church agreed to keep out of politics.

The Nazis believed concessions were temporary and later attempted to co-ordinate the **Catholic Youth**.

The German Faith Movement

As an alternative to Christianity, the Nazis established a **Teutonic paganism**, which:
- upheld a racial belief based on blood (descent) and soil (homeland)
- replaced Christian ceremonies with pagan ones
- rejected Christian ethics
- upheld Hitler's **cult of personality**.

Church and state relations

By 1935, the Nazis had failed to co-ordinate the Churches and there was growing opposition within them. It was a problem for the Nazis, as suppression would alienate many Germans, but limited persecution allowed Churches some independence.

The Ministry of Church Affairs adopted policies to undermine the Church. It closed some Church schools, removed crucifixes from others, banned nativity plays and carols from schools and undermined Catholic Youth groups. Campaigns were launched to harass and discredit the clergy: some, such as Niemöller and Bonhoeffer, were sent to concentration camps, while others were simply prevented from teaching religious classes. Church funds were confiscated, making it harder for the Church to function. However, the popularity of priests such as Bishop Galen, who attacked the policy of euthanasia, leading to its official suspension, made it difficult for the Nazis to take further action.

At the start of the war, the regime wanted to avoid unrest. However, with initial German military success, the persecution of the Churches was increased, particularly in the conquered regions.

Success?

Nazi religious policy had limited success, as only 5 per cent of Germans joined the German Faith Movement. The Churches did compromise to preserve their organisations, and there was some sympathy with Nazism because of traditional values and the dislike of communism.

⚬ Spectrum of significance

Below are a question and a list of general points that could be used to answer the question. Use your own knowledge and the information on the opposite page to reach a judgement about the importance of these general points to the question posed. Write the numbers on the spectrum below to indicate their relative importance. Having done this, write a brief justification of your placement, explaining why some of these factors are more important than others. The resulting diagram could form the basis of an essay plan.

> 'The main reason for the failure of the Nazi policy towards the Churches was the strength of Christian beliefs within Germany.' How far do you agree?

1   The strength of Christian belief within Germany
2   The actions of individual churchmen
3   The lack of support for the German Faith Movement
4   The Nazis' willingness to compromise with the Churches
5   Limited persecution did not destroy the Churches
6   The outbreak of war resulted in a more cautious policy being adopted.

←──→

Least important   Most important

⚬ Develop the detail   a

Below are a sample exam question and a paragraph written in answer to this question. The paragraph contains a limited amount of did the Churches successfully resist Nazi policies towards them?

> The Churches were quite successful in resisting Nazi policies. Although some Protestant churches supported and helped the Nazis. However, the attempt to reorganise the Protestant churches failed and other Protestant leaders did resist and established their own Church, independent of the state. The Catholic Church wanted its independence and reached an agreement with the regime, but later the Nazis attempted to ignore the concessions. To overcome the problems, the Nazis tried to establish an alternative to Christianity, but this also failed. Policies to undermine the Church were also adopted by the Nazis, but it was hard for the Nazis to take much action and their policies had only limited success.

Economic policy

A major reason why the Nazis came to power was the economic problems that Germany faced since the First World War, particularly those caused by the Great Depression. Hitler had gained much of his support by claiming he would solve the problem of unemployment, which stood at 6 million in 1932.

Schacht's economic strategy

Hjalmar Schacht was a financier, president of the Reichsbank, 1933–39, and minister of economics, 1934–37. To bring about recovery, he followed a policy of public investment, largely by the state, which spent heavily. This resulted in a policy of **deficit financing**. He adopted the following policies:
- setting interest rates at a low level
- rescheduling the debts of local authorities
- giving assistance to farmers and small businesses
- introducing public works, such as public building, motorways, land reclamation and reforestation.

As a result, government expenditure rose by 70 per cent from 1933 to 1936. Unemployment fell and although fears about inflation did not materialise, a **balance of trade deficit** did occur, as Germany imported more raw materials and failed to increase its exports, which meant the country was short of money.

Schacht's New Plan

A debate over where money should be spent, either on consumer goods or rearmament, led to the appointment of Schacht. He introduced the 'New Plan' in September 1934:
- The plan gave the government control over all trade, tariffs, capital and currency exchange.
- The government decided which imports were allowed, with priority given to heavy industry.
- Bilateral trade treaties were signed, particularly with south-east Europe.
- Germany bought goods on the condition that the Reichsmarks were used to buy German goods.
- **Mefo bills** were introduced.

However, the plan only hid the balance of payment problem, and by 1936 this was getting worse. Schacht wanted to reduce arms expenditure and increase the production of industrial goods to sell. This resulted in the **'guns or butter'** debate.

Göring's Four Year Plan

The problem was resolved by bringing in the **Four Year Plan** under **Hermann Göring** in 1936. It aimed to increase rearmament and **autarky** so that Germany was self-sufficient in food and industrial production. The plan aimed to:
- increase agricultural production
- increase the production of raw materials
- develop **ersatz** products
- control the labour force to prevent inflation
- regulate imports and exports in favour of rearmament at the expense of agriculture.

Schacht resigned as economics minister in 1937 and was replaced by Walther Funk, although it was Göring who really held power. Although production rose in some industries, such as aluminium, it did not reach the targets for oil or rubber, and failed to meet the levels required by the armed forces. When war broke out, Germany still relied on foreign supplies for one-third of its raw materials.

Although the German economy was dominated by preparations for war, it was not ready for **total war**.

The position of workers

Schacht's policies led to a reduction in unemployment, which fell to 1.6 million by 1936, in part due to job creation schemes, but also the introduction of conscription in May 1935. As a result, many workers supported his policies and the party.

Although unemployment fell, workers lost many rights, as independent unions were banned and replaced by the German Labour Front or DAF (*Deutsche Arbeitsfront*), which was under Nazi control and the only option available to workers. Workers also lost the right to negotiate wages and conditions of work, which were arranged through the DAF, which supervised conditions and dealt harshly with unrest.

The regime attempted to win the support of workers through the 'Strength through Joy' movement (KdF or *Kraft durch Freude*), which offered workers sports facilities, cultural visits and holidays, but in practice these were only available to loyal workers.

Despite the problems, many were simply happy to have a job, even though:
- Real wages only surpassed 1929 levels in 1938.
- Working hours rose from 43 hours in 1933 to 47 in 1939.
- Those working in consumer industries struggled.

! Spot the mistake

Below are a sample exam question and a paragraph written in answer to this question. Why does this paragraph not get into Level 3? Once you have identified the mistake, rewrite the paragraph so that it displays the qualities of at least a Level 3. The mark scheme on page 7 will help you.

How successful were the Nazi economic policies from 1933 to 1939?

In September 1934, Schacht brought in his New Plan, which aimed to give the government control of the economy and prevent large amounts of imports. Schacht's economic policy involved signing bilateral trade deals with countries in south-east Europe, such as Romania and Yugoslavia. These deals were often barter agreements. He also introduced Mefo bills, which were like credit notes. They were guaranteed by the government as payment for goods. The policy also involved Germany purchasing raw materials from countries if they used the money to buy back German goods.

i Turning assertion into argument

Below are a sample exam question and a series of assertions. Read the question and then add a justification to each of the assertions to turn each one into an argument.

To what extent was the German economy ready for war in 1939?

The German economy was not prepared for a long war in 1939 because

_____

_____

However, the Four Year Plan under Göring did help to overcome some problems because

_____

_____

Despite this success, there were still problems because

_____

_____

The Nazi view of women

The Nazis believed that women should look after the family and the home. Women were expected to have large families, as a growing population was a sign of strength and was needed to supply soldiers. Women had a completely different role to men, and were expected to be devoted to the 'three Ks': *Kinder, Küche, Kirche* (children, kitchen, church).

Under the Weimar Republic, not only had women gone out unaccompanied, drunk and smoked in nightclubs, but more had taken up employment and the birth rate had dropped. The Nazis wanted to reverse both trends.

The ideal Nazi woman

The ideal Nazi woman was blonde, athletic and fit, with big hips, which were seen as better for child-bearing. She was expected to:
● not smoke
● avoid the use of make-up
● wear clothes with full skirts and flat shoes
● be a good cook and be able to use leftovers, and to make a one-dish meal at least once a month.

Nazi policies to 1937

In June 1933, women were offered interest-free loans of 600 Reichsmarks to marry and give up work. **Labour exchanges** were encouraged to discriminate in favour of men. Women were excluded from politics. The Nazi Women's Organisation was established to put across **anti-feminist ideology**.

In January 1934, the proportion of girls allowed to enter higher education was limited and this was extended in 1937. **Grammar school** education for girls was abolished and they were banned from studying Latin, a requirement for university.

Nazi policies after 1937

From 1937, Nazi policies had to change because:
● There was a labour shortage.
● The Four Year Plan required more workers.

As a result, women were required for factory work and they were allowed to rejoin the professions. The number of working women rose from 5.7 million in 1937 to 7.1 million in 1939; the number of female doctors also increased and girls were encouraged to become teachers. Women in work were also allowed marriage loans.

War also meant women were needed for work, and by 1942, 52 per cent of the workforce was female. Women also took on military responsibilities as **auxiliaries**, manning searchlights and anti-aircraft batteries.

The family

The Nazis took a series of measures to increase the size of families. This included strict anti-abortion laws and limited contraception advice. They also improved maternity benefits and family allowances, gave marriage loans worth half a year's salary for each child, and reduced taxes in proportion to the number of children in a family.

A propaganda campaign raised the status of motherhood through rewards such as the 'Mother's Cross', which was given in bronze, silver or gold, depending on the number of children you had. Nazi policies culminated with the slogan, 'I have donated a child to the Führer'.

Lebensborn was introduced in 1935 to improve 'racial standards'. Under this policy, unmarried mothers of 'good racial background' were cared for, and Aryan girls were impregnated by members of the SS. Around 11,000 children were born under this policy.

Success?

Although the birth rate increased, this may have been due to the end of the Depression. Marriage figures did not increase and divorce rates actually rose. It could be argued that the status of women increased as the role of the mother was seen as important, but women were denied many opportunities.

Complete the paragraph a

Below are a sample exam question and a paragraph written in answer to this question. The paragraph contains a point and specific examples, but lacks a concluding explanatory link back to the question. Using the information from the opposite page, complete the paragraph, adding this link in the space provided.

How successful were Nazi policies towards women?

One of the major aims of Nazi policy was to take women out of work so that they could stay at home and look after large families. In the period up to 1937, women were discouraged from working and incentives were provided, such as loans to encourage marriage, while labour exchanges were encouraged to discriminate in favour of men. Employment opportunities for women in many of the professions, such as the medical profession or high ranks of the civil service, were also limited. However, with a labour shortage in 1937, the Nazis had to go against their ideals and recruit women to work in factories, and this process was further developed as a result of Germany's decision to go to war because of the shortage of labour.

_____

_____

_____

_____

Develop the detail a

Below are a sample exam question and a paragraph written in answer to this question. The paragraph contains a limited amount of detail. Annotate the paragraph to add additional detail to the answer.

'The Nazi policy towards women brought them many benefits.' How far do you agree?

In order to achieve the Nazis' goal of a larger population, women were expected to have large families. In order to achieve this, the Nazis introduced incentives for women to marry and offered benefits if they had large numbers of children. At the same time, a propaganda campaign raised the status of motherhood, and further rewards were given to women depending on the number of children they had. However, whether some of the measures to increase the size of families should be seen as bringing benefits is a matter of debate. Although the woman's role was seen as different to that of men, the Nazis argued that they improved women's status. However, many would argue that they were denied many opportunities.

Education and youth

Education

The Nazis wanted to use education to consolidate the Nazi system and **indoctrinate** the youth with Nazi ideals. In order to achieve these aims, teachers had to reinforce Nazi beliefs and values.

How did the education system change?
- Schools were centralised under the Reich Ministry of Education, Culture and Science.
- '**Unreliables**' were removed from the teaching profession.
- Courses were organised for non-Nazi teachers.
- Head teachers had to be members of the Nazi Party.
- A National Socialist Teachers League was established.
- The curriculum was changed.

Curriculum changes

More time was given to PE, as strength and fitness were essential for producing soldiers. There was increased emphasis on German and History, as these emphasised nationalism and heroism. Biology reinforced Nazi **racial genetics** and the population policy (see page 44). Meanwhile, Religious Studies was dropped as Christianity was seen as unimportant. The Nazis also created schools to produce the Nazi elite:
- The Napolas – state boarding schools run by the SS
- Adolf Hitler schools run by the Hitler Youth
- *Ordensburgen* – a type of school designed to produce the elite for Hitler's future society.

What were the results?

There were many failures in the education programme:
- The Nazis opened few new schools.
- The anti-academic ethos in schools resulted in a fall in standards, which caused resentment, and the professional classes chose to send their children to grammar schools rather than **Nazi schools**.
- The numbers joining the teaching profession declined, as many disapproved of Nazi ideology.

Hitler Youth

Hitler Youth is the term used to describe a range of youth groups in Germany (see Table 2.2 below). The Nazis wanted to use the Hitler Youth to indoctrinate the young, as they were the future of the regime. Membership grew from 1 per cent of youth in 1933 to 60 per cent in 1936, and became compulsory in 1939. The Nazis also dissolved all other youth groups, except the Catholic Youth movement.

▼ Table 2.2 Hitler Youth groups

Age	Male	Female
10–14	*Deutsches Jungvolk* (German Young People)	*Jungmädel bund* (Young Girls League)
14–18	*Hitlerjugend* (Hitler Youth)	*Bund Deutscher Mädel* (League of German Girls)

Activities

Boys' activities emphasised the role of a soldier. Girls were taught the roles of a wife and mother through domestic activities. Both received political indoctrination – German **patriotism** and the achievements of Hitler were emphasised. With the outbreak of war, youth groups had to help with the harvest, and there was increased military training.

Success?

Many from poorer backgrounds enjoyed the activities. However, the Hitler Youth lost some appeal when it was made compulsory and increased its military emphasis. Some of those disillusioned with the Hitler Youth set up the Edelweiss Pirates and the Swing Youth (see page 34).

! Support or challenge? a

Below is a sample exam question which asks you how far you agree with a specific statement. Below this are a series of general statements that are relevant to the question. Using your own knowledge and the information on the opposite page and the previous page, decide which general statements support or challenge the statement in the question and tick the appropriate box in each case.

'Nazi education policy was concerned only with teaching military values.' How far do you agree?

	Support	Challenge
There was great deal of emphasis on PE in the Nazi curriculum.		
Girls were taught the importance of being healthy.		
Racial studies formed a key part of the Nazi curriculum.		
In the Hitler Youth, much time was devoted to marching, camping and hiking.		
History lessons were largely about German history from the First World War.		
Nazi ideology was taught in both schools and the Hitler Youth.		
Maths lessons were often based around the angles of missiles and projectiles or the bombing of Jewish ghettoes.		
Religious education was dropped from the curriculum.		
The Nazis allowed the Catholic Youth movement to survive.		

i Introducing an argument

Below are a sample exam question, a list of key points to be made in the essay, and a simple introduction and conclusion for the essay. Read these and then, using the information on the opposite page and page 34, rewrite the introduction and the conclusion in order to develop an argument.

Assess the reasons why the Nazi Party was so concerned about the education of young people in Germany.

Key points:
- They were the future of the 1,000-year Reich.
- The young were the soldiers of the future.
- The young were very impressionable.
- Girls had a particular role to play in Nazi Germany.
- Teachers could influence the young about Nazi ideals.
- Education could stress the success of the Nazi Party and the greatness of Germany.

Introduction:

There were many reasons why the Nazi Party was so concerned about education in Germany. These reasons were linked to the future of Germany and the indoctrination of the young, as well as the roles they had to play. It is important to consider the role that they would have to play in the future and why the Nazis were so concerned about education. All of these factors help to explain why they were so concerned.

Conclusion:

To conclude, there were many reasons why the Nazi Party was so concerned about education. These reasons link to the future of Germany and the role that young people had to play. The likelihood of war was an important factor, as was the need to increase the population. However, the most important reason was the role the young would play.

Racial policies to 1939

At the centre of Nazi ideology was the idea of a 'racially pure state'; therefore, some groups of people were excluded from the *Volksgemeinschaft*. Those excluded were considered to be 'biologically inferior' or subhuman (*Untermenschen*), and of 'lesser racial value'. They were discriminated against and persecuted.

This ideology was based on **Social Darwinism** and the survival of the fittest. The Nazis believed:
- Aryans (*Herrenvolk*) were the superior race because of their intelligence, hard work and willingness to make sacrifices for the nation.
- Germany had lost the First World War because of the weak, so they had to be removed.
- Mixing with *Untermenschen* had contaminated the Aryans. To achieve racial purity, selective breeding and removal of undesirables was needed.

Policies

The Nazis introduced the following range of policies against those who did not fit the Nazi ideal:
- A propaganda campaign against undesirables to create resentment
- A Sterilisation Law in 1933: the Law for the Prevention of Hereditary Diseased Offspring, which allowed for the sterilisation of the 'simple-minded', 'chronic alcoholics' and sufferers of schizophrenia, hereditary blindness and deafness. From 1934, about 350,000 men were sterilised
- The Law against Dangerous Habitual Criminals, 1933, which introduced compulsory castration for certain sexual offenders
- A department within the Gestapo to deal with homosexuality – a law was introduced in 1935 which led to the arrest of 50,000 homosexuals
- By 1936, the **work-shy**, tramps, beggars, prostitutes, homosexuals and juvenile delinquents were sent to concentration camps
- The euthanasia campaign, 1939, by which the Nazis started to exterminate the mentally ill and killed 5,000 handicapped young. By 1941, protests forced the programme to be stopped. It was restarted in secret and extended to foreign workers with incurable physical illnesses, racially inferior babies and terminally sick prisoners
- Asocials were put into forced labour.

Gypsies

Gypsies were persecuted as non-Aryan, work-shy and homeless. The Nazis feared they would mix with Aryans. As a result:
- In 1935, gypsies were banned from marrying Germans.
- In 1938, a 'Decree for the Struggle against the Gypsy Plague' was issued. Under this decree, gypsies were registered to ensure racial separation.
- In 1939, 30,000 gypsies were deported to special sites in Poland.

Jews

Nazi policy went through three phases:
- Origins: the development of Nazi ideology.
- Gradualism: during 1933–39, there was legal discrimination, terror, violence and forced emigration.
- **Genocide** (see page 52).

Anti-Semitism: origins and gradualism

Anti-Semitism was not new, and in the nineteenth and early twentieth centuries, Jews had been portrayed as inferior to the German race. This view developed as Germans looked for scapegoats to explain their defeat in the First World War and the economic crisis of the 1920s and early 1930s. The Nazis used this to develop an anti-Semitic ideology.

Legal discrimination

Laws gradually removed Jewish rights, supported by propaganda, posters and newspapers (*Der Stürmer*) and films (*The Eternal Jew*).

Measures:

1 April 1933	**Boycott** of Jewish shops – this was not widely accepted
7 April 1933	Law of Restoration of the Professional Civil Service, excluding Jews from the civil service
1935 Nuremberg Race Laws	Jews lost their citizenship, and marriage between Jews and Germans was forbidden
1938	Jewish doctors not allowed to practise
1938	Polish Jews expelled
1938	Jews excluded from schools and universities
1938	Compulsory closure and sale of Jewish businesses

Violence

From 1934 to 1938, violence was localised and sporadic. However, in March 1938, there were attacks on 200,000 Jews in Vienna. On 9–10 October, a co-ordinated campaign across Germany, known as Kristallnacht, was launched. Jewish homes, businesses and synagogues were attacked and approximately 100 Jews were killed.

Emigration

In 1938, the Central Office for Jewish Emigration in Vienna was established, under Adolf Eichmann, to force Jews to emigrate, followed by the establishment of the Reich Central Office for Jewish Emigration in 1939. About half the Jews left before the war.

! Mind map

Make a copy of the mind map below and use the information on the opposite page to add detail. Add information about Nazi policies towards these groups and their reasons for persecuting them.

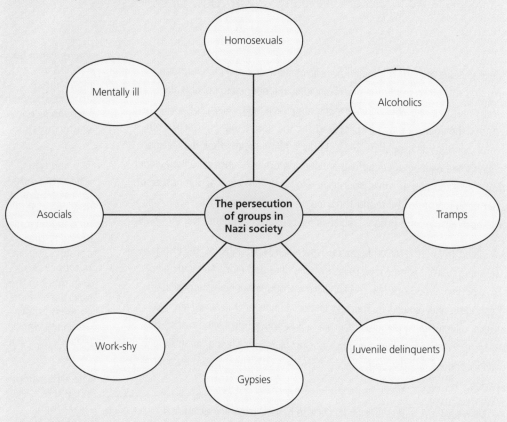

⬩ Eliminate irrelevance a

Below are a sample exam question and a paragraph written in answer to this question. Read the paragraph and, using the information from the opposite page, identify parts of the paragraph that are not directly relevant to the question. Draw a line through the information that is irrelevant and justify your deletions in the margin.

How popular were Nazi policies towards the Jews in the period from 1933 to the outbreak of the Second World War?

It could be argued that many of the Nazi policies towards the Jews in this period were popular. They were, after all, only exploiting the Germans' desire for a scapegoat for their problems, particularly defeat in the First World War and the economic crisis. However, some policies, such as the euthanasia programme aimed at the mentally ill, provoked criticism from Church leaders and were abandoned. The popularity of the policies can be seen in events such as Kristallnacht, when, according to many accounts, there was a spontaneous attack on Jewish homes, businesses and synagogues. However, in contrast, the policies adopted during the Second World War were not always popular, with many ordinary Germans sheltering Jews, even if members of the SS were willing to commit atrocities. Yet the lack of support for events such as the boycott of Jewish businesses in April 1933 suggests that even those policies were not popular and that policies were simply accepted because people were forced to conform or were subject to propaganda.

Exam focus

REVISED

Below are a sample exam question and a model answer. Read the question, and then the answer and the comments around it.

'Hitler's economic policies failed to prepare Germany for war.' How far do you agree?

Hitler developed economic policies specifically aimed at rearmament and making Germany a self-sufficient country and therefore ready for war. However, the economic policies did not exploit Germany's full potential, and although Germany may have been ready for a short, relatively small war in 1939, the country was not prepared for the actual war that broke out, and certainly not the total war that developed in 1942. Hitler's plans meant that the German war economy could be sustained only by successfully conquering other countries, which would allow Germany to exploit the resources of other countries. However, because of the nature of German rearmament, Germany would not be ready for a major war until the mid-1940s. This was in stark contrast to both Britain and France, which were prepared economically by 1939.

The New Plan of 1934 aimed to be stricter on imports. This aided Germany's preparation for war, in so far as Germany would become less reliant on imports and more self-sufficient, preparing the nation for wartime conditions. Mefo bills were introduced, which successfully disguised government spending and allowed further expansion. However, the New Plan was only a short-term measure, which simply disguised Germany's economic problems rather than preparing the economy for war. Indeed, balance of payment problems increased, even though industrial production had increased 60 per cent since 1933, and GDP had grown by over 40 per cent in the same period.

In 1936, the Four Year Plan was introduced. Its aims were to have Germany's army and economy ready for war within four years. The Four Year Plan was successful to some extent, as by 1939, 10,000 aircraft had been built. However, this was only a small increase in production, as between 1933 and 1935, Germany had produced 8,000 planes. Moreover, the increase was tiny compared to Britain, which had been able to treble its production in the same period. Consequently, production failed to reach the levels necessary to prepare Germany for war. The plan also failed to make Germany self-sufficient. Under the Four Year Plan, demand for imports did not increase, but stood at the same level as before the introduction of the plan. Germany had been reliant on imports before the plan, and it appeared that with the failure to decrease the levels, this remained the situation, which was not ideal during wartime. As a result of this situation, Germany had failed to meet its aim of self-sufficiency, and as a consequence was unprepared for war. Arms production had not reached the levels required by Hitler and the army and, similar to self-sufficiency, increased production had not been met.

There was a growing demand for consumer goods, which led Schacht, who had been responsible for the New Plan, to believe that cuts to arms production needed to be made. However, this was unacceptable to Hitler and led to the 'guns or butter' debate. The plan was a success in so far as consumption levels dropped by 20 per cent, and production in a number of key industries, such as aluminium and explosives, expanded. However, the plan failed to meet targets in the key industries of rubber and oil, and arms production was well short of Hitler's targets. Reliance on imports did not increase, but it was still not reduced, and this meant that when war did break out, Germany still relied on imports for one-third of its raw materials.

The introduction establishes a clear line of argument, which focuses directly on the question.

The opening sentence could be stronger and more directly focused on and linked to the actual question, but there is an argument in the next part which suggests that Germany was preparing for war.

The discussion about the New Plan is balanced, with the argument that it did not succeed, and this is well supported with precise and accurate facts.

The paragraph concludes with an interim judgement, having considered both sides, a feature of higher-level responses.

The discussion about success is balanced and a conclusion based on the discussion is reached.

The success of Blitzkrieg in the period 1939–1941 suggests that the economy was prepared for war. However, when total war broke out, this was far from the case. Some historians, such as Tim Mason, would argue that this was far from the case even before 1942. There were already growing shortages in raw materials, food and consumer goods, and with labour shortages, wages were rising, increasing pressure on the economy, which was already becoming difficult to finance and, according to Mason, may have been a reason for going to war in 1939, believing it would be a short war of conquest. Moreover, if Germany was not prepared for war in 1939, it was certainly not prepared for total war in 1942. Although Speer's 'total war' economy did result in a rapid increase in ammunition by 97 per cent, tanks by 25 per cent and arms production by 59 per cent in six months, the economy could not compete with the production of the USA or the USSR. Therefore, although Speer was successful in increasing production levels, he ultimately failed to meet those needed for war.

The outbreak of war in 1939 had not helped German preparation, as many projects were due to be completed by 1942–43. This situation was made even worse by Allied bombing and the diversion of resources to construct anti-aircraft installations and underground sites. As a consequence, Germany was unable to achieve a total war economy, which would have made the country more prepared economically for war; but even when arms production did peak in August 1944, it was still well below its full potential. The Nazi economy had been incapable of meeting the demands of either a war of conquest, as it failed to exploit the conquered territories, or total war fully.

Germany was not prepared for war in 1939, or for the total war that developed in 1942. Not only had earlier economic policies failed to provide the armed forces with the resources they needed, but even when a total war economy was adopted, it still failed to reach full production and Germany was never able to match the levels of production of the Allied countries. The early successes of Blitzkrieg only masked the fundamental problems of the economy, despite the apparent achievements of both the New Plan and the Four Year Plan.

A clear idea is offered in the opening sentence and this view is developed and debated throughout the paragraph.

Historiography is not a requirement of this paper, but the response makes good use of the knowledge of the debate, bringing in the Mason thesis, but it is used to take the argument forward, rather than simply describing it, which would gain no credit.

A well-developed judgement, which follows from the rest of the essay, is reached. It has been well supported and therefore makes the overall argument convincing.

The argument in the paragraph is developed and supported.

Throughout the essay the answer is well supported by appropriate and accurate detailed knowledge of levels of production; significantly, the evidence is used to support the argument and not simply described. The answer covers the whole period from 1933 to 1945, as the question is drawn from two key topics, which can happen. Candidates often fail to cover the whole timescale. Some of the opening sentences could have been better linked to the actual question and introduced an idea, rather than describing policies. The conclusion supports the line of argument adopted in the rest of the essay. Despite some shortcomings, the answer is focused and does analyse the main issues to reach a balanced judgement and therefore would reach the higher levels.

Reverse engineering

In order to reach the very top level, candidates need to reach judgements about the issue they are considering in relation to the question. Identify the paragraphs where the candidate has successfully done this, and those where a judgement is either absent or not developed. In the latter case, write a couple of sentences for each of the paragraphs so that a judgement based on the argument is reached.

2 The establishment of the Nazi dictatorship and its domestic policies, February 1933 to 1939

Exam focus

Below are a sample short-answer question and a model answer. Read the question, and then the answer and the comments around it.

Which was of greater importance in establishing the Nazi dictatorship?

(i) The Enabling Act
(ii) The Night of the Long Knives
   Explain your answer with reference to both (i) and (ii).

The Enabling Act, passed in March 1933, was crucial in establishing the Nazi dictatorship, as it transferred full legislative powers to the chancellor, Hitler, and his government for four years, thus establishing a dictatorship. This Act therefore meant that parliament and parliamentary legislation became an irrelevance, with the Reichstag virtually voting away its own existence. However, in actually voting it away, rather than having it imposed by force, it gave the establishment of a dictatorship the appearance of legality, even though members of the Reichstag had been intimidated to ensure its passage. The Act also helped to strengthen Hitler's position within the Cabinet, as the president's approval was no longer needed for passing legislation, further adding to Hitler's power. It also gave Hitler the power to revise the constitution and removed any doubts that the middle classes had about the legality of the Nazi takeover, as everything appeared to have been done legally.

> The significance of the Enabling Act is clearly explained.

> The response offers a number of reasons why the Act was important and these are fully expanded and developed.

The Night of the Long Knives in 1934 secured Hitler's position within his own party, as it removed the potential opposition of the SA and its leader Röhm, who wanted the Nazi revolution to become more radical. The destruction of the SA also pleased the army, who had feared the SA, but now supported Hitler with Blomberg's public vote of thanks; and it led to the personal oath of loyalty to Hitler that the army took a few months later, thus removing the one group that might oppose him. It also removed many of the traditional politicians such as Schleicher, who might have opposed some of his policies. Most importantly, it secured Hitler's personal supremacy, as his decisions were accepted and he had been able to legalise murder, showing clearly that the regime was a personal dictatorship and he could get away with anything.

> A reason is clearly identified and explained.

> A further reason is explained and this is fully developed, with good detailed knowledge.

Although both events were important in establishing the Nazi dictatorship, the Enabling Act was more significant as it enabled Hitler to embark on a policy of co-ordination, or *Gleichschaltung*, and create the one-party state by early 1934. This allowed Hitler to remove potential opposition in nearly every walk of life, including trade unions and other political parties; thus it was more significant in removing a range of opposition than the Night of the Long Knives. The only exception to this was the army, and the Night of the Long Knives was the event that won Hitler their support, but this simply completed the task begun by the Enabling Act. It is also unlikely that Hitler would have been able to undertake the Night of the Long Knives without the power and confidence he had gained from the Enabling Act, which again suggests that the Enabling Act was the most important event, as it was the basis of the dictatorship and helped take Hitler from the position of chancellor to that of Führer.

> There is even some suggestion as to judgement about the most important aspect of the feature being discussed.

> A clear view as to the most important event is identified and there is some explanation.

> The judgement continues to be developed and there is further comparison.

> The judgement is further developed and there is a comparison between the two events.

The response analyses and evaluates both factors thoroughly. The supporting knowledge is detailed and accurate, and this allows a developed judgement to be reached, based on the evidence in the two main paragraphs. The answer would therefore be placed in the higher levels.

Reverse engineering

In order to reach the higher levels, you must reach a judgement as to which event was the more important. This response argues that it was the Enabling Act. Use the information in the answer to rewrite the conclusion to argue that the Night of the Long Knives was more important in establishing the Nazi dictatorship.

3 The impact of war and defeat on Germany, 1939–49

The war economy and total war

REVISED

During the 1930s, Hitler had pursued an increasingly aggressive foreign policy. Initially, he had just taken back German land taken away by the Treaty of Versailles, but with the failure of the British and French policy of appeasement he gained confidence, which was further reinforced by a treaty with Russia. This allowed him to attack Poland in September 1939, which resulted in the outbreak of war in Europe.

The growth of the Nazi economy

German victories at the beginning of the war, as a result of **Blitzkrieg**, suggested that the economy had not been overstrained. However, this is challenged by Nazi aims and economic figures:

- Economic decrees were issued in December 1939, which outlined vast programmes for war production.
- German military expenditure more than doubled in the period 1939–41.
- Food rationing was introduced at the start of the war for some goods.
- Clothes rationing was introduced in November 1939.
- Soap was rationed and toilet paper was not available.
- The labour force was mobilised for war.
- Civilian consumption declined.
- Despite this, armaments production was low:
  - The number of planes increased from 8,290 in 1939 to 10,780 in 1941.
  - The number of tanks for the invasion of Russia in June 1941 was only 800 more than for the invasion of the west.

Production was hit by inefficiency and poor co-ordination. The problem was made worse by a lack of central control, as there were numerous agencies. There were Ministries of Armaments, Economics, Labour and Finance, all with different interests and demands.

As a result, by 1941, economic mobilisation for total war had failed to achieve the required levels of armaments production.

Total war

By the end of 1941, Germany was at war with Britain, the USSR and the USA, but armaments production was lower than in Britain. In response, in December 1941, Hitler issued the **Rationalisation Decree**.

In February 1942, **Albert Speer** was appointed minister of armaments. He introduced a policy of 'industrial self-responsibility' to ensure mass production. In April 1942, a Central Planning Board was set up; this was supported by a range of committees, which represented different parts of the economy. Speer co-ordinated the production process and ensured that resources were exploited. As a close friend of Hitler, he was able to exert influence and he introduced a number of important policies:

- Prisoners in concentration camps were used as workers.
- Women were employed in arms factories.
- Skilled workers were no longer conscripted.
- Anything that did not contribute to the war effort was eliminated:
  - Professional sport was ended in March 1943.
  - Magazines not essential to the war were closed.
  - Non-essential businesses were shut.

Was Speer's policy a success?

At first, Speer's policy appeared to be successful. In the first six months:

- Tank production rose by 25 per cent.
- Ammunition production rose by 97 per cent.
- Total arms production increased by 59 per cent.

By 1944, there had been a threefold increase in war materials since 1942.

However, the economy could have produced more and was handicapped by a number of factors:

- Party Gauleiters had influence at local level and could prevent Speer's orders being carried out.
- The SS did as they wanted and exploited lands for personal gain.
- Conquered territories were not exploited economically.
- The impact of Allied bombing (see page 52).

The Nazi economy was unable to meet the demands of total war. Production levels peaked in August 1944, but were below their potential.

⚡ Develop the detail   a

Below are a sample exam question and a paragraph written in answer to this question. The paragraph contains a limited amount of detail. Annotate the paragraph to add additional detail to the answer.

How successful was Germany in developing its economy for war?

The early victories in the war suggested that the German economy was well prepared for war. Hitler had been determined to avoid the problems faced by Germany in the First World War, and therefore prepared thoroughly for all aspects of war production. Despite this, the policy was not successful in a number of ways and economic mobilisation was limited. The problems were made worse by organisational issues, which meant there were groups with different interests. In the period when Speer first came to power, however, there appeared to be an improvement, and war production rose until later in the war. However, the levels could have been even higher, but were limited by a number of factors, with production peaking in June 1944, but never reaching its potential.

⚡ Support your judgement

Below are a sample exam question and two basic judgements. Read the exam question and the two judgements. Support the judgement that you agree with most strongly by adding a reason that justifies the judgement.

'Germany was never able to achieve a total war economy.' How far do you agree?

Overall, Germany failed to achieve a total war economy and could have produced much more.

_____

_____

Under the economic ministry of Speer, Germany was able to reach unprecedented levels of production and came close to a total war economy.

_____

_____

Bombing

Air raids against Germany began in 1940, and by 1942 they had become more frequent and intense. As they became more intense, many left the cities and moved to rural areas. The attack on Hamburg in 1943 caused a firestorm which killed 30,000 people, and emergency services were unable to cope. The government was forced to build emergency accommodation. The intensity increased in 1945, and up to 150,000 were killed in raids on Dresden, with 70 per cent of properties destroyed. Nearly as many civilians were killed by bombing as the number of soldiers who were killed fighting.

What was the impact of the bombing?

The blanket-bombing of German cities has been condemned since the war, and some historians have questioned its effectiveness because economic production figures show that it failed.

However, it can be argued that bombing prevented Germany from reaching its full economic potential, caused industrial destruction and a breakdown in communications. Germany was forced to move workers to construct anti-aircraft batteries and underground sites, which further limited production.

Morale

Despite the bombing and, from 1943, the awareness that defeat was likely, morale remained good and people carried on fighting until the surrender in May 1945. Historians have suggested a number of reasons for this:
● Some shared Hitler's belief that he would establish a 1,000-year Reich.
● The Gestapo forced people to keep fighting.
● Some believed that Germany would develop a super-weapon and win the war.
● As in Britain, with the Blitz, bombing united people.

Anti-Semitism: genocide

The German occupation of Poland in 1939 brought 3 million Jews under Nazi control. War made resettlement difficult and therefore **ghettoes** were created.

1941

In June 1941, following the invasion of Russia, SS *Einsatzgruppen* followed the invading army and rounded up Jews. They carried out mass shootings, murdering 700,000 Jews in 1941–42. From September 1941, Jews had to wear the yellow Star of David, so they could be easily identified. The practical problem of fighting the war and dealing with the number of Jews resulted in the Nazi leadership finding a '**final solution**'.

The final solution

The final solution was agreed at the **Wannsee Conference** in January 1942. The policy had changed from resettlement to extermination. The final solution outlined plans to use gas for extermination, and resulted in the development of extermination centres at Auschwitz, Sobibor and Treblinka. Jews were moved from the ghettoes to death camps. The whole process became like an industry, as the camps were located near railway lines to speed up the transportation. In 1943, the Warsaw ghetto was destroyed and the Jews were transported to death camps. In 1944, Jews from all over German-conquered lands were transported to death camps, which were located away from Germany. As a result, over 6 million Jews were killed, along with political opponents, homosexuals, Jehovah's Witnesses, gypsies, anti-socials and even Russian prisoners of war.

Was the final solution planned?

There is much historical debate as to whether the final solution was planned from the start.

Those who uphold this argument believe that Hitler was committed to the extermination of the Jews from early in his career and followed a consistent policy of gradually increasing persecution, resulting in extermination, because that is what he wanted. Some historians have even suggested that the Holocaust was intended because many Germans took part in it.

However, an examination of events suggests that the implementation was haphazard, as there were no written orders for the killing of the Jews. This suggests that the policy was only decided at the end of 1941 and agreed at Wannsee in January 1942.

ⓘ Recommended reading

As the final solution is an area of great historical debate and is part of the topics that could be set for the AS Level interpretation question, it is worth spending some time studying it in some depth, as it will enhance your understanding of the debate. Below is a list of suggested further reading on this topic.

- Michael Burleigh, *The Third Reich* (2000)
- Michael Burleigh and Wolfgang Wippermann, *The Racial State: Germany 1933–45* (1991)
- Mary Fulbrook, *Collins Flagship Historymakers: Hitler Book 2*, pages 46–60 (2005)
- Daniel Goldhagen, *Hitler's Willing Executioners* (1996)
- John Hite and Christopher Hinton, *Advanced History Core Text: Weimar and Nazi Germany*, pages 340–56 (2000)
- Geoff Layton, *Access to History: Democracy and Dictatorship in Germany 1919-63*, pages 241–8 and 262–6 (2015)

ⓘ Use own knowledge to support or contradict ⓐ

Below is an interpretation about the final solution. You are asked to summarise the interpretation, then use your own knowledge to agree and then to contradict.

'The final solution came to be implemented as a result of the chaotic nature of government within the regime. Various institutions and individuals improvised a policy to deal with the military and human situation in Eastern Europe by the end of 1941.'

Adapted from: Geoff Layton, *Germany: The Third Reich 1933–45* (1992)

Summary:

_____

_____

_____

Agree with the interpretation:

_____

_____

_____

Contradict the interpretation:

_____

_____

_____

Hitler committed suicide at the end of April 1945, and a new government briefly took over and signed an unconditional surrender on 8 May 1945. The Allies now took over joint control of Germany.

The Potsdam Conference

The Allies agreed to divide Germany into four zones at the Yalta Conference in February 1945. They met again at Potsdam in July 1945. This conference was attended by Soviet leader Stalin, US President Truman and British Prime Ministers Churchill and Attlee. There were disagreements between Russia and the other Allies over boundaries and reparations, which helped form a divided Germany in the long term.

What was agreed?

- Germany was to be administered under joint Allied control and was divided into four zones of occupation, as was Berlin.
- Germany was to be demilitarised, de-Nazified and democratised.
- Elections were to be held, starting at a local government level, to give Germany the 'chance to rebuild its life on a democratic and peaceful basis'.
- Poland gained much former German land; the Oder–Neisse line formed the border between Poland and the Soviet zone.
- Germans in Poland, Hungary and Czechoslovakia were repatriated to Germany.
- The economy was to be run as one unit, and each occupying force was to take reparations from their zone of occupation.
- As the Soviet zone had fewer resources, they were allowed an additional 25 per cent of reparations from the British and American zones.

The Soviet zone

Demilitarisation

German forces disbanded after their surrender in May 1945. As there was no German government, there could be no independent German military force. This remained the case until 1955.

De-Nazification

The Nazi Party was disbanded and major war criminals were tried at Nuremberg. The Soviet zone interned large numbers of former Nazis, many of whom died in the former concentration camps where they were held. Later, 'normal' Nazis who committed themselves to communism returned to political life. The Soviets argued that Nazism resulted from capitalism, therefore capitalism had to be destroyed:

- Large landed estates were confiscated and redistributed among landless agricultural labourers.
- Former Nazis' property was taken; some was kept by the state.
- A similar process was adopted later for banks and factories.
- Some equipment was dismantled and taken back to Russia as reparations. Russia also removed experts to reconstruct technical equipment in Russia.

Democratisation

German communists, led by Walter Ulbricht, arrived in Berlin at the end of April 1945. They planned to gain control in Berlin, but give the appearance of democracy.

The Soviet Military Administration (SMAD) issued Order Number 2 on 10 June 1945, which licensed the formation of political parties. All parties were brought together in an anti-fascist bloc, or National Front, against Nazism in July 1945.

The KPD, or Communist Party, was established, followed by the Social Democratic Party (SPD). These were merged in 1946 to form the Socialist Unity Party (SED). The SPD distrusted communist policy and its links with the army, but agreed to unite as they saw it as the only way for them to influence policy.

Liberal parties also merged to form the Liberal Democratic Party of Germany (LPD). The Catholic Centre Party and Protestant parties formed the Christian Democratic Union (CDU).

At first, it appeared as if the Communist Party would adopt a democratic approach, but by 1948 it had formally abandoned democracy.

Simple essay style

Below is a sample exam question. Use your own knowledge, the information on the opposite page and information from other sections of the book to produce a plan for this question. Choose four general points, and provide three pieces of specific information to support each general point. Once you have planned your essay, write the introduction and conclusion for the essay. The introduction should list the points to be discussed in the essay and outline the line of argument you intend to take. The conclusion should summarise the key points and justify which point was the most important.

'The communists had no intention of allowing democracy to develop in the Soviet zone in the period 1945–49.' How far do you agree?

Turning assertion into argument ⓐ

Below are a sample question and a series of assertions. Read the exam question and then add a justification to each of the assertions to turn each one into an argument.

'The main aim of the Soviets was to win popular support through their policies.' How far do you agree?

Economic policies were a significant method of winning popular support because they led to

_____

_____

However, in many instances, the Soviets were more concerned with exploiting their zone economically because

_____

_____

Also, Russia took away technical experts to Russia because

_____

_____

The consolidation of the SED and developments in the Soviet zone

The SED was the leading communist party in the East, led by Walter Ulbricht. It claimed to be a liberator from fascism and argued that ordinary workers and peasants were innocent of Nazism and war guilt. Property belonging to absentee factory owners, Nazis, war criminals and **Junkers** was confiscated. This helped the SED to win popular support.

The founding statement of the SED claimed it was wrong to impose the Soviet system and called for 'the establishment of an anti-fascist, democratic regime, a parliamentary-democratic republic'.

Initially, the Communist Party encouraged the development of parties with which they could work, but the SED increasingly gained control of other parties in the Soviet zone and set up two new parties, the National Democratic Party, aimed at former Nazis, and the Democratic Peasants Party of Germany, aimed at peasants.

All parties agreed that state control and economic intervention were needed, and this gave communist plans and the Communist Party further support.

How did the communists dominate the Eastern zone?

Initially, the Communist Party did not have mass support and could not control all areas of life. In some areas of East Germany, non-communists were appointed as mayors. However, the communists ensured that they did control education and the appointment of personnel, so as to build up a group of reliable supporters in key areas and ensure that future generations were educated in communist principles.

- Having gained popular support, the communist SED gradually eliminated other political groups and views.
- The Soviet military command suppressed political party activity in Berlin. CDU and LDPD activities were ended.
- Free expression was severely limited and political dissent was restrained.
- The military government determined appointments and dismissals.

Democracy was formally abandoned in 1948–49, and the SED announced a **Marxist–Leninist** 'Party of a New Type'. It was based on the principle of **democratic centralism**. It also established 'mass organisations' under communist control of youth, women and unions in the Soviet zone.

! Support or challenge?   a

Below is a sample exam question which asks you how far you agree with a specific statement. Below this are a series of general statements that are relevant to the question. Using your own knowledge and the information on the opposite page and the previous page, decide which general statements support or challenge the statement in the question and tick the appropriate box in each case.

'The communists never intended the DDR to remain democratic.' How far do you agree?

	Support	Challenge
Elections were to be held in Germany, starting at a local level.		
A range of political parties were established in the Russian zone.		
Communists were to be in charge of personnel and education.		
Not all mayors were communists.		
All parties were brought together in a 'National Front'.		
Mass organisations were put under communist control.		
Liberal and religious parties were allowed.		
The Soviet military command suppressed political party activity in Berlin.		
The National Democratic Party and the Democratic Peasants Party of Germany were established.		

i Developing an argument   a

Below are a sample exam question, a list of key points to be made in the essay, and a paragraph from the essay. Read the question, the key points and the sample paragraph. Using the information from the opposite page and from page 54, rewrite the paragraph in order to develop an argument. Your paragraph should explain why the factor discussed in the paragraph is either the most significant factor or less significant than another factor.

'The control of key appointments was the most important reason why the communists were able to dominate the Soviet zone.' How far do you agree?

Key points:

- The SED had popular support.
- State control and economic intervention were needed.
- Communists controlled key appointments.
- Mass organisations under the communists were established.
- Developments in the Western zone.

> The control of key appointments was a factor in enabling the communists to dominate the Soviet zone. The communists did control education. The control of education meant that the young would be educated in communist beliefs. The communists also controlled the appointment of key personnel. The appointment of key personnel gave the communists a group of reliable supporters in important areas. The communists also established mass organisations for women, trade unions and young people. The SED also won popular support because of its economic policies, as the property of factory owners, former Nazis and landowners was seized.

The Western zone, 1945–49

At Yalta and Potsdam, the Allies had agreed to keep a single state, yet they had different concepts of its social, economic and political organisation.

Problems in the Western zone

Germany suffered total defeat in 1945, with occupation and massive territorial losses. Following its surrender, Germany ceased to exist as a state and had to be administered by the Allies. There were three Western zones – British, French and American – and this was repeated for Berlin. The Allied Control Council (ACC) was the military governing body, whose decisions had to be unanimous, and when this failed, each military governor could implement decisions in their zone, which resulted in different policies in each zone.

There were severe economic problems, which could better be addressed by greater co-operation between the zones.

Problems following the Second World War included:
- food and fuel shortages
- homelessness
- bereavement
- integration of soldiers into civilian society
- refugees
- dealing with the impact of genocide
- the collapse of the currency.

Events in the Western zone

The timeline below outlines the developments towards greater unity within the Western zone.

1946

The USA drew up plans for German reconstruction, but Russia and France did not agree. France did not want a strong Germany and wanted large reparations; it even annexed the Saar for a short period.

1946–47

A severe winter worsened conditions. A weak British economy, with bread rationing at home, meant Britain was unable to fund its zone.

1947

By 1947, economic recovery was essential to prevent an economic crisis and social revolution in Western Europe. Food had to be imported, which cost $700 million per year. The problem was made worse as some industry had been dismantled to pay reparations and there had been an influx of refugees. The British and American zones were merged to form **Bizonia**. Aid was poured into the Western zone.

1948

The **Marshall Plan** was applied to the Western zone. The **London Conference**, between February and June 1948, agreed a West German currency and state. From summer 1948 onwards, Western representatives of the '**Parliamentary Council**' started to devise a constitution for a new state in the West.

1949

France, after initial resistance, joined the British and American zones and created **Trizonia**. A new constitution, the **Basic Law**, was adopted in May 1949, which established a West German state.

The growing divisions between the East and West zones

In 1947, economic problems resulted in the British and American zones being merged to form Bizonia. The French joined in 1949 to form Trizonia. Disputes developed over Soviet reparations from the Western zones. There was also growing division between Russia and the West over the **Truman Doctrine** and **Marshall Aid**.

A black market had grown in the West due to the weakness of the currency; the introduction of a new currency, the Deutschmark, was essential before aid was brought in. However, the Soviets refused to follow suit, and, antagonised by this decision, they began the Berlin blockade, which confirmed the division of Germany. Russia stated that 'technical difficulties' – the reason it gave for the blockade – would continue until plans for a West German government were abandoned. The Russians also brought in their own currency, the East German mark.

! Support or challenge? a

Below is an exam-style question which asks you how far you agree with a specific statement. Below this are a series of general statements that are relevant to the question. Using your own knowledge and the information on the opposite page and the previous page, decide which general statements support or challenge the statement in the question and tick the appropriate box in each case.

'Economic difficulties were the most serious problem in the Western zone.' How far do you agree?

	Support	Challenge
There were severe food and fuel shortages in the Western zone.		
There had been a large influx of refugees from the East.		
The Western zone had suffered large-scale damage during the war.		
The new government had to overcome the impact of Nazi rule and genocide.		
The structure of the ACC and the need to achieve unanimous decisions created difficulties.		
There were divisions between France, the USA and Great Britain.		
The weakness of the British economy meant the British were unable to support their zone.		
The weakness of the German currency and the resultant black market created economic problems.		
Inflation severely damaged the economy in the Western zone.		

! Delete as applicable a

Below are a sample exam question and a paragraph written in answer to this question. Read the paragraph and decide which of the options (in bold) is the most appropriate. Delete the least appropriate options and complete the paragraph by justifying your selection.

'Economic difficulties were the greatest problem facing the Western zones in the period 1945–49.' How far do you agree?

To a **great/fair/limited** extent, economic problems were the greatest difficulty facing the Western zones in the period 1945–49. **Most/some/few** of the economic difficulties were due to the legacy of the Second World War. This was particularly true with issues such as food shortages and homelessness. These problems lasted a **long/short** time and were made worse by difficulties in Britain, which could not fund its zone. These problems got **better/worse** by 1947 and **support/challenge** the view that it was difficulties from the war that were the main issue. The situation was also **helped/not helped** by the attitude of **France/Russia/ France and Russia**. To a **great/fair/limited** extent, the economic problems were overcome only when Trizonia was formed and a new currency introduced. However, it was the attitude of Russia towards the Western zones that was the greatest problem for the Western zones because

_____

_____

The Cold War and the Berlin blockade

The Berlin blockade was the single most important event in confirming the division of Germany into two countries, East and West Germany. However, in many ways, it was the occasion rather than the cause of the division.

Although the West and East had been Allies during the war, they were united only by their hatred of Hitler and desire to defeat him. It was therefore not surprising that difficulties, which had been apparent during the war, continued to develop into the **Cold War**.

Traditional historians have argued that Stalin wanted to spread Communism in his bid for world domination, and therefore the seizure of the whole of Berlin was part of that process. Revisionist historians have argued that the Cold War was the result of US fears of communism and that the Soviet economy was in no position to expand or become involved in further conflict.

The Berlin blockade was the culmination of developments, not just within Germany. The USSR appeared to be expanding its influence, having taken control of many states in Eastern Europe, and Churchill argued that an '**Iron Curtain**' had come down.

In response to communist expansion, the US President Truman issued the Truman Doctrine, promising to support governments against communism. The USA also believed that communism spread to countries where there was a poor standard of living, and therefore offered material resources to help reconstruct the economies of countries with the Marshall Plan, which the Soviets refused to accept.

Events

From June 1948 to 12 May 1949 – as a result of growing divisions between the Western Allies and the Soviets, particularly over currency (see page 58) – the Soviets blocked access to West Berlin. The Soviets blocked all transport links by rail, road, air or waterway. They aimed to starve West Berlin and force its merger into the Soviet zone.

The Allies supplied West Berlin through Berlin's Tempelhof airport, bringing in food, medical supplies and fuel. They also built a new airport in the Tegel area of French Berlin. This showed the Soviets that they would not relinquish control of the Western zone. West Berlin became a symbol of resistance to the spread of communism and confirmed the division of Germany.

Impact

The West was now concerned to protect Western democracy from communism and stop West Berlin falling to the Soviets, without a war. Berlin became the centre of the Cold War.

ⓘ Turning assertion into argument   a

Below are a sample question and a series of assertions. Read the exam question and then add a justification to each of the assertions to turn each one into an argument.

To what extent was the West to blame for the Berlin blockade?

The actions of the Western powers within their zone were to blame for the Berlin blockade because

_____

_____

However, the East precipitated the action because

_____

_____

Also the East's attitude towards currency reform was crucial because

_____

_____

ⓘ Use own knowledge to support or contradict

Below is an interpretation to read about the Berlin blockade. You are asked to summarise the interpretation, then use your own knowledge to agree and then to contradict.

'The crisis was planned in Washington behind a smokescreen of anti-Soviet propaganda. The conduct of the Western powers risked war. The self-blockade of the Western powers hit the West Berlin population with harshness.'

Adapted from: a Soviet commentary on the crisis, quoted in Peter Fisher, *The Great Power Conflict* (1985)

Summary:

_____

_____

_____

Agree with the interpretation:

_____

_____

_____

Contradict the interpretation:

_____

_____

Exam focus

Below are a sample exam question and a model answer. Read the question, and then the answer and the comments around it.

How far were the Western powers to blame for the division of Germany in 1949?

The division of Germany in 1949 would have been unthinkable before the Second World War, which suggests that it was the outcome of the war and those who were responsible for the war who were responsible for the division in the long term. However, that ignores the roles played by the Allies, particularly in the years between 1945 and 1949. The Western powers of America, Britain and France, through their economic policies in particular, were at least partially to blame for the division. However, the role of the Soviets and their apparent desire to expand westward and spread Communism cannot be ignored. Yet in the short term, it was disagreements over their various zones of occupation and their economic treatment that led to the final division and the creation of two separate German states.

In the long term, Nazi Germany must take some of the responsibility for the division of Germany in 1949. The regime had started the war and it was its failed policy of military expansionism that brought the Western powers and the Soviet Union into Central Europe in 1945, ensuring that decisions about the future of Germany were not made by the German people, but by the Allied forces who now occupied the country.

The Western leaders, Churchill and Attlee and Roosevelt and Truman, played a significant role in the division of Germany. In the wartime conferences at Tehran, Yalta and Potsdam, they were unable to agree with the Soviet leader, Stalin, about the future of Germany. However, although their ideological, political and economic differences with Stalin were partly to blame, so was the attitude of the Soviet leader. His desire to exploit all the economic potential of Germany to pay for the cost of the war created divisions among the Allies, as America, in particular, wanted to restore the economic prosperity and stability of Germany, so that it became a trading partner and did not become unstable. Stalin must also share at least some responsibility for the division because of his desire for security for the Soviet Union. Having been invaded twice in the century, he was determined to secure a buffer zone for the Soviet Union, even though it meant occupying parts of Eastern Europe, which caused concern among the Western powers, which therefore looked to strengthen democracy and their control and influence over their own areas in Germany. However, it was not just Stalin, but Truman who was also responsible for creating tensions, which would result in the divisions. His perception of Soviet intentions resulted in America adopting policies which appeared to be ever more hostile towards the Soviet Union. Most importantly, the Truman Plan and Marshall Aid were clear statements that America intended to contain Communism and prevent its spread in Western Europe. This had serious implications for the zones of occupation in Germany, as it meant that America would aid the economy of the zones in the west, which America, Britain and France occupied. Similarly, the Americans also made it clear that they would use troops to defend these zones actively from any Russian advance. As a result, through their policies, the Americans had made the restoration of German unity very unlikely.

The decisions made by the Allies at the end of the war meant that co-operation was unlikely, and both the West and the USSR were therefore responsible for the subsequent division. The requirement that the Allied Control Council required unanimity to make decisions made co-operation very difficult. At the same time, the different sides were unable to agree on how to meet the costs of the occupation of Germany. It meant that by 1946, the military governors of the zones, in order to try to overcome the economic chaos into which areas had sunk, were making their own decisions, based more and more on the interests of their own country and

The opening sentence puts forward a possible explanation for the division.

However, the answer is aware that there is a debate about the reasons for the division and offers another possible reason.

The opening is focused, and by offering another possible main reason shows an awareness of the main issues for debate.

The opening sentence offers a view as to the most important reason for the division.

The paragraph starts with a balanced discussion about the roles of the individuals.

The opening sentence introduces the idea which is directly related back to the question.

the people within the zones. As a result, divisions were already apparent, and this became even more apparent when Britain, unable to fund its zone, merged with the American zone to form Bizonia. It was therefore circumstances and mistakes in the way that the ACC was established that reinforced divisions between the two sides and made division more likely.

German politicians also played a key role in the division of Germany. German politicians worked with Allied leaders who shared their views. As a result, in the Eastern zone, Ulbricht and members of the SED worked with the communists, while in the West, Adenauer, Erhard and the CDU worked with America and Britain. This development simply reinforced divisions and was seen most clearly at the conference of representatives of all German *Länder* at Munich in 1947, when they were unable to agree on an agenda. As a result, German politicians should also take some of the blame for the subsequent division.

However, in the short term, it does appear as if the West must take most of the responsibility. The need for economic revival in Germany required currency reform, as the current currency, the Reichsmark, created instability. The West, despite knowing that Russia would oppose currency reform, pushed it through and introduced it to their three zones in June 1948. Moreover, the West kept their plans secret from Russia, even producing the new notes and coins in America to maintain the secrecy. The Russians viewed it as an attempt to undermine their zone and saw it as contrary to the unanimity required by the ACC, and therefore they made plans to bring in their own currency. With the establishment of two separate currencies, the actual political division was a step closer. Although a new currency was essential for economic stability, given inflation and the thriving black market, the management of its introduction and the animosity it created with Russia were the fault of the West.

The new currency also prompted a major crisis over Berlin, which ultimately led to the division of Germany. Although the West was responsible for the currency crisis, Russia's response with the Berlin blockade completed the division. However, it was the occasion rather than the cause of the division. Long-term issues and tensions had meant that unity was unlikely. The currency crisis brought that division to the brink, but the blockade sealed it. Although Stalin hoped that the blockade would lead to an end to the new currency and the surrender by the Western powers of their zones in Berlin, it had the opposite effect. The blockade and airlift helped to unite the Western Allies and many Germans, with the result that Berlin became officially divided. Russia had raised the tensions over Berlin and ultimately triggered the division, but Western actions over currency reform had brought matters to a head.

In the long term, ideological divisions and the different priorities of the Allies meant it would be difficult to keep Germany united. However, in the short term, it was economic issues that caused the division. The West had certainly not helped, as it created Bizonia, and introduced the Marshall Plan and the new currency. But Russia must also take some responsibility, as it had also brought in a new currency and nationalised land and industry, which went against the economic beliefs of the West.

A supported judgement is reached about the decisions, in which both sides must share responsibility.

As with the previous paragraph, an idea directly related to the question is introduced.

An interim judgement is reached about the role of the factor discussed.

Following detailed discussion, a judgement is reached which is based on the discussion in the main body of the paragraph.

The opening sentence offers a view on the impact of currency reform, which is again linked back to the question.

The discussion about the blockade is balanced.

The conclusion has a clear judgement and is balanced.

The answer would reach the highest level, but not the very top. Some of the interim judgements could be developed, and in places, some of the supporting material could be more detailed and precise. The impact of the Berlin blockade on the division might be explored further.

Reverse engineering

Use the comments and the mark scheme in order to move the response to the very top of Level 6, making a list of the additional features that would enable the answer to achieve full marks. Remember, it does not have to be perfect, but an answer that is a best fit with the descriptors.

Exam focus

Below are a sample AS Level interpretation question and a model answer. Read the question, and then the answer and the comments around it.

'The outbreak of war and its subsequent escalation into total war seriously weakened the Jews' chances of survival. Any "resettlement plans" had now become a major logistical and bureaucratic operation, the size of which helped to tip the scales in favour of physical annihilation.'

Adapted from: Volker Berghahn, *Modern Germany* (1987)

Evaluate the strengths and limitations of this interpretation, making reference to other interpretations that you have studied.

The interpretation puts forward the view that the final solution of the Jewish question was largely the result of the outbreak of the Second World War and its subsequent escalation, arguing that it 'seriously weakened' the Jews' chances of survival'. The interpretation suggests that resettlement became much more difficult because of the war and therefore it 'tipped the scales in favour of physical annihilation'. This contrasts with other views that have suggested that Hitler had a long-term aim to destroy and annihilate the Jews, and this can be traced back to *Mein Kampf* and was therefore not dependent on the outbreak and escalation of war. This view sees Hitler's policies towards the Jews gradually becoming more severe, and suggests that they led logically from the limited persecution of 1933 to the death camps of places such as Auschwitz.

It is true that with the outbreak of war in September 1939, the nature of the Jewish problem changed dramatically for the Nazi government. War increased the number of Jews under Nazi control and this did weaken their chances of survival, as there were so many of them that resettlement became much harder, particularly after the invasion of Russia in 1941. The interpretation is correct that war undermined resettlement plans, as plans to settle Jews in occupied Poland were abandoned by Göring in March 1940, and then plans to use Madagascar, a French colony and island in the Indian Ocean, had to be abandoned because Britain was unwilling to make peace and the Royal Navy controlled the ocean. The plans for the invasion of Russia and the build-up of troops also made the idea of reverting to resettlement in Poland very difficult, and once the invasion of Russia took place and the war became a racial and ideological war designed to destroy Jewish bolshevism, annihilation became even more likely. Moreover, during a war, the interpretation is correct to stress that it would be a bureaucratic nightmare to resettle people, as they would need to be fed and housed, whereas the main concern of Germany would have been to fight the war, and this became even more important when victory was not quick and all resources were required for that. The interpretation stresses that annihilation may have been an unforeseen consequence of the war and, given the absence of any similar policies before the war, this view has its strengths. The role of the war in determining the policy would also fit with the number of Nazi orders that were being issued for the extermination of the Jews by 1941, whereas such plans had been absent before.

The interpretation is clearly explained and this allows the response to identify key areas that can be examined for strengths and limitations.

The interpretation is placed in the wider context of the debate about the extermination of the Jews.

The alternative view is explained succinctly and this will allow the response to use these ideas to examine the limitations of the interpretation.

A strength of the interpretation is identified and own knowledge is used directly to confirm it.

A second area of strength is explained by using own knowledge about the problem of resettlement once the war had started.

This pattern continues and a further area of possible strength is considered.

The response adds to the strength of the answer by considering a good range of issues raised by the interpretation.

However, the interpretation ignores the fact that policies towards the Jews had been gradually increasing in severity, and that with events such as Kristallnacht in 1938, the regime was already becoming more severe before the outbreak of war. This escalation can also be seen with the passing of the Nuremberg Laws, which helped to enforce the hatred of Jews. Ensuring there was support for his policies would be a slow process, and the interpretation ignores this and the fact that Hitler would have needed time to win people over to such a policy, although it could be argued that war would speed this up and make such a policy more acceptable. Therefore the interpretation ignores the idea that pressure was already increasing on the Jews in Germany and that, even in 1938, Hitler informed Göring that the Jewish question should be solved. He also made a speech to the Reichstag in January 1939, in which he stated that if war broke out, it would lead to the annihilation of the Jews. The problem with these statements is whether they should be believed, although it could be that Hitler was warning that they might be murdered if necessary if war broke out.

A range of limitations is examined and precise evidence is used to explain these.

The discussion, however, is balanced, and the response notes that war might make such a policy more acceptable.

Further evidence for limitations to the interpretation are given and directly linked back to it.

The response is able to place the interpretation in the wider context of the debate about the origins and reasons for the Holocaust. The response does not get sidetracked, however, by considering the different schools of thought, which is not needed to reach any level. The strengths and weaknesses of the interpretation are considered, and the supporting knowledge is detailed and accurate. The interpretation is evaluated and there are clear examples of linking own knowledge to the actual interpretation to do this. As a result, it would reach the highest level.

The answer is aware that there are problems with some of the evidence, suggesting that the overall response is balanced.

Reverse engineering

The key to a good answer is to evaluate the given interpretation and use your own knowledge to show the strengths and limitations of the interpretation. Go through the response and identify all the evaluative words that are used in the answer.

4 Divided Germany: the Federal Republic and the DDR, 1949–63

The Basic Law and the constitution of West Germany

REVISED

In May 1949, a new constitution, the Basic Law, was adopted, and in August 1949, **Konrad Adenauer**, leader of the Christian Democrats, was elected chancellor.

The main features of the Basic Law were:
- Freedom of expression, assembly, association and movement were guaranteed.
- It established a 'representative democracy', whereby popular participation is limited to voting every few years and the public merely selects who will rule for them. This kept power in the hands of the elite to prevent the emergence of another Hitler.
- Federal state: individual states kept much power over regional issues, and at a national level they were represented in the upper chamber (**Bundesrat**).
- The lower chamber (**Bundestag**) was elected by a complex system which combined proportional representation with **first past the post**. It was later added that parties had to gain 5 per cent of the vote before they were represented. This was done to prevent the emergence of small, extremist parties.
- The law was to be temporary until Germany was united. It committed Germany to work for unity and all Germans living in former German lands were allowed citizenship. All those who left the **DDR** were able to settle and work in the West.
- All parties had to uphold democracy. Extremist parties that were not committed to parliamentary democracy were banned. This prevented anti-democratic parties from gaining a majority.
- The president was not directly elected, but was chosen by a representative convention. This prevented an anti-democratic leader. The powers of the president were limited, largely formal and symbolic, and prevented rule by decree.
- The chancellor was appointed by the president, but needed parliamentary approval. The chancellor could not be dismissed unless a new chancellor was voted in, which prevented the president from appointing and dismissing a chancellor at will. The proposed chancellor had to have parliamentary support; otherwise, new elections had to be called.

At first, there were many small parties in West Germany, but gradually the numbers declined. This was because:
- The constitution banned far-right and far-left parties.
- From 1953, the 5 per cent hurdle at federal level prevented smaller parties from gaining representation in the Bundestag. In 1957, the number of constituencies that had to be won was raised from one to three.
- Small parties were divided.
- Many right-wing groups joined the CDU (see page 68).
- There were social changes (see page 74).

De-Nazification

There was a mass internment of former Nazis who had political responsibilities and leadership roles. The Allies wanted to remove Nazis from all positions in society, but it proved to be impracticable. Therefore, in 1946, they decided to deal with de-Nazification on a case-by-case basis. Penalties were harsh and resulted in people playing down their Nazi past. Some obtained **affidavits** to show they were clear. It did not help Germany confront the past. When the German authorities took over the role, many escaped punishment, some because they were useful in an anti-communist role.

Mind map

Make a copy of the mind map below and use the information on the opposite page to add detail to it.

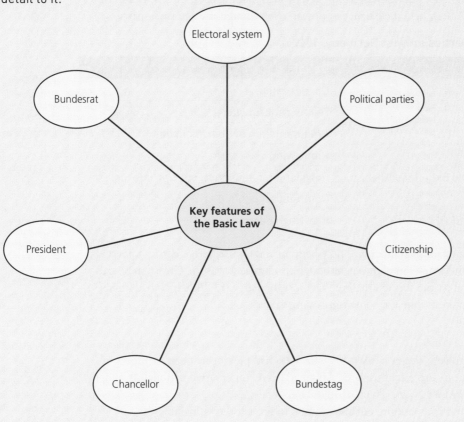

Key features of the Basic Law

- Electoral system
- Bundesrat
- Political parties
- President
- Citizenship
- Chancellor
- Bundestag

Develop the detail　a

Below are a question and a paragraph written in answer to this question. The paragraph contains a limited amount of detail. Annotate the paragraph to add additional detail to the answer.

'The main aim of the Basic Law was to prevent democracy from being undermined by constitutional means.' How far do you agree?

There were many elements of the Basic Law that were designed to prevent a repeat of 1932–33. Political parties had to support the system and those that did not were banned. The president was not voted for by the people and his powers were limited. The chancellor had to be approved by parliament and could not simply be dismissed by the president. The voting system was designed to prevent small parties from being represented, and the combination of two electoral systems also ensured that more extreme parties were unlikely to gain seats.

Political parties and elections

In 1945, the Allies allowed the formation of political parties, and four major parties and some smaller ones emerged. By 1949, politics was dominated by two main parties: the CDU and the SPD. However, the FDP often held the balance of power, even though it was a small party.

▼ Table 4.1 Political parties in West Germany, 1949

Party	Beliefs
Christian Democrats (CDU/CSU)	Conservative
Social Democratic Party (SPD)	Democratic-Socialist
Free Democratic Party (FDP)	Amalgamation of liberal parties
German Party (DP)	Right-wing
League of Refugees and Expellees (BHE)	Revisionist, nationalist, special-interest
Communist (KPD)	Communist: banned in 1956
Socialist Reich Party (SRP)	Pro-Nazi: banned in 1952

The SPD and KPD were established quickly. The Christian and Conservative Parties joined to form the CDU (Christian Democratic Union), although in Bavaria it was the Christian Social Union (CSU). The liberal parties formed the Free Democratic Party (FDP), which had liberal principles and business interests, but also some right-wing views.

The CDU

The Christian Democrats were conservative Christians who had previously been members of the Catholic Centre Party or Protestant parties. Many had been conservative nationalists under Weimar and some were former Nazis. The Christian Democrats:
- supported capitalism and competition, but also wanted to protect the vulnerable
- supported the welfare state
- followed the Ahlen Programme, which outlined beliefs in traditional Christian values, a social conscience and the free market (in 1957, this was replaced with centre-conservative policies).

The SPD

The Social Democrats were a traditional socialist party. They appealed to workers. The Social Democrats:
- had been formed from Marxist and working-class movements
- abandoned Marxism in 1959, at the Bad Godesberg Conference
- wanted social justice combined with individual freedom.

Elections and election results

From 1949 to 1963, Konrad Adenauer was Chancellor of Germany and presided over a series of coalition governments. Because of his control and power over his own government ministers, his period in power is often referred to as **chancellor democracy**. It was also a period when elections were little more than a series of plebiscites in favour of the government. It has been argued that it removed popular self-government. However, it did ensure responsible self-government.

▼ Table 4.2 Election results in West Germany, 1949–61

Year	CDU/CSU		SPD		FDP		KPD		Others	
	%	Seats	%	Seats	%	Seats	%	Seats	%	Seats
1949	31	139	29.2	131	11.9	52	5.7	15	22.2	65
1953	45.2	243	28.8	151	9.5	48	2.2	0	14.3	45
1957	50.2	270	31.8	169	7.7	41	–	–	10.3	17
1961	45.3	242	36.2	190	12.8	67	–	–	5.7	0

Simple essay style

Below is a sample exam question. Use your own knowledge, the information on the opposite page and information from other sections of the book to produce a plan for this question. Choose four general points, and provide three pieces of specific information to support each general point. Once you have planned your essay, write the introduction and conclusion for the essay. The introduction should list the points to be discussed in the essay and outline the line of argument you intend to take. The conclusion should summarise the key points and justify which point was the most important.

'The most important reason for the disappearance of opposition to Adenauer was the organisation of the political system in West Germany.' How far do you agree?

Turning assertion into argument   a

Below are a sample question and a series of assertions. Read the exam question and then add a justification to each of the assertions to turn each one into an argument.

'Popular self-government disappeared in West Germany under Adenauer.' How far do you agree?

It could be argued that popular self-government disappeared in Germany under
Adenauer because

_____

_____

However, the period can also be described as a chancellor democracy because

_____

_____

Yet elections could be seen as irrelevant because

_____

_____

The West German economy and the economic miracle REVISED

Food production in 1947 was only 51 per cent of that in 1938, and industrial output only 38 per cent. Initially, the Allies prevented the rebuilding of the German economy and even dismantled the German steel industry. Reparations took away $10 billion, which damaged the economy further.

However, there was a gradual realisation that unless the German economy recovered, the European economy could not recover, and in the 1950s, there was what has been described as an economic miracle.

Industrial production rose (see Table 4.3 below), resulting in higher wages; incomes went up 400 per cent between 1949 and 1963. Growth rates for GNP were about 8 per cent in the 1950s. Meanwhile, unemployment fell from 8.1 per cent (2 million) in 1950 to 0.5 per cent in 1965.

Why was there an 'economic miracle' in the West?

Recovery started with the creation of Bizonia in 1947 (see page 58) and with economic policies introduced before 1949, such as:

● removing price controls, which stimulated business by allowing free competition between private enterprises
● removing controls over wages and production, allowing workers a role in management and decision-making, which resulted in fewer strikes
● ending inflation through currency reform
● reducing marginal tax rates, so that those on higher incomes had more money to spend on goods.

These policies encouraged people to work and were reflected in a decline in absenteeism. In Bizonia, the index for industrial production had risen from 51 per cent in June 1948 to 78 per cent by December.

The West also had a number of advantages, as it possessed raw materials, had not suffered as much damage in the war as was feared, and had not had as many reparations taken as in the East. The work ethic of the population and the availability of cheap labour from the East meant that the West could meet the demands of the occupying forces.

Further stimulus was provided by Marshall Aid, although historians now question its importance. It had brought in only $2 billion by October 1954, and in 1948–49 provided less than 5 per cent of German national income. The Germans were also paying reparations and restitution payments to the Allies.

The Korean War (1950–53) increased the demand for goods the Ruhr could supply. This was helped by the fact that other nations were unable to supply war materials, with the result that exports doubled.

Government policies may also have helped, although historians disagree on this. Ludwig Erhard developed the 'social market economy', combining government legislation and capitalism to produce 'prosperity for all'.

The economic recovery helped to provide political stability. As a result, Adenauer remained in power from 1949 until his resignation in 1963.

▼ Table 4.3 Growth in production levels from 1950 (1950=100). The statistics show the growth rates, with 1950 as the baseline. Figures over 100 indicate the percentage increase, and figures below 100, the percentage decline.

Year	All industry	Mining	Consumer goods	Food
1951	109.6	107.2	108	113.8
1952	114.2	112.4	110.8	121.4
1953	122.1	114.8	118.9	124.6
1954	132.4	118.6	128	134.2
1955	138.3	126.9	138	145
1956	144.5	132.1	144.7	150.5
1957	155.1	138.9	157.4	158.9
1958	163.1	145.4	166.9	167.3
1959	179.8	158.1	186.1	180.5

⚠ Delete as applicable   **a**

Below are a sample exam question and a paragraph written in answer to this question. Read the paragraph and decide which of the options (in bold) is the most appropriate. Delete the least appropriate options and complete the paragraph by justifying your selection.

'Economic policies introduced before 1949 were the most important reason for the recovery of the West German economy.' How far do you agree?

To a **great/fair/limited** extent it was the economic policies introduced before 1949 that brought about the West German economic recovery. **Most/some/few** of the policies helped to stimulate the economy, and a reduction in taxes helped as people had **more/the same/less** to spend on goods, which **encouraged/discouraged** production. These policies **encouraged/discouraged** people to work and this was seen in an **increase/decrease** in absenteeism. However, it was not just the decisions made before 1949 that were important, as the Korean War played a crucial role because

_____

_____

⬍ Support your judgement

Below are a sample exam question and two basic judgements. Read the exam question and the two judgements. Support the judgement that you agree with most strongly by adding a reason and detail that justifies the judgement.

'Marshall Aid was the most important reason for the West German economic miracle.' How far do you agree?

Marshall Aid played a crucial role in stimulating the West German economy

_____

_____

_____

_____

The role of Marshall Aid in the recovery of the West German economy has been exaggerated.

_____

_____

_____

_____

Foreign policy: integration with the West

Economic integration

International organisations were established to prevent Germany from waging war again, and to manage the potential of the German economy. However, they became part of the movement for Western European integration. Adenauer made West Germany indispensable to the West, made sure it was a member of these organisations and rejected closer relations with the East.

October 1949

West Germany joined the Organisation for European Economic Co-operation (**OEEC**) and received Marshall Aid.

April 1951

West Germany joined the European Coal and Steel Community (**ECSC**). This placed Franco-German production under a common authority and started European economic unity. This removed foreign control over West German industry, provided it with equal status as a member state and helped reconciliation with France.

1957

West Germany signed the **Treaty of Rome**, which established the European Economic Community (**EEC**), later the EU. In the same year, West Germany joined **EURATOM** (European Atomic Energy Community), a sign of increased trust and the success of Adenauer's policies.

Political integration

The **Council of Europe** was established in 1948. Adenauer joined and stated, 'We belong to the West, not to Soviet Russia'. He accepted the division of Germany and renounced any independent initiative for West Germany, which reassured France.

Military integration

NATO was established in 1949, and West Germany joined in 1955. NATO asked West Germany to contribute forces to the Korean War, a sign of growing trust, although this concerned France.

Adenauer achieved German rearmament within Europe through NATO, and NATO forces were placed on German soil. West Germany also agreed not to seek reunification by force.

Relations with the USSR

These developments concerned Stalin, and in 1952 he contemplated giving up the DDR for a united, neutral Germany. However, Stalin insisted that a democratic and united Germany could not join Western powers, because of his concerns about security.

Adenauer ignored all advances from Russia. He also ignored the 1953 rising in East Berlin (see page 76). However, he did visit Moscow in 1955 and negotiated the return of former prisoners of war (POWs).

Adenauer did not recognise East Germany as a separate state, and refused to have diplomatic relations with countries that did. This was known as the **Hallstein Doctrine** and was not abandoned until the 1970s.

Was Adenauer's foreign policy a success?

Success

- West Germany achieved *rapprochement* with France.
- Germany's reputation in Western Europe was rebuilt.
- West Germany negotiated the return of POWs from Russia in 1955.
- West Germany joined the OEEC, ECSC, EEC and NATO.
- Adenauer oversaw the 1957 plebiscite for the reincorporation of the Saar into Germany.
- West Germany was treated as an equal, unlike post 1919.

Failure

- Adenauer was never able to reconcile the USSR to German rearmament.
- The remilitarisation of German society and the creation of a German army created fear at home.

Develop the detail a

Below are a question and a paragraph written in answer to this question. The paragraph contains a limited amount of detail. Annotate the paragraph to add additional detail to the answer.

How successful were Adenauer's attempts to integrate West Germany into European affairs?

> Adenauer's attempts at integration were successful. He was able to convince European powers of his peaceful intentions and achieved a good relationship with his Western neighbours through various European organisations, acknowledged in his recovery of lost land. West Germany was at the forefront of many European organisations designed to bring about economic integration, and later political organisations. The country became trusted militarily and developed its own forces. However, these achievements were at the expense of better relations with the East, although there were some successes. Adenauer would not recognise a divided Germany and gave little support to those Germans cut off from West Germany.

RAG – rate the timeline

Below are a sample exam question and a timeline. Read the question, study the timeline and, using three coloured pens, put a red, amber or green star next to the events to show:

- Red – events and policies that have no relevance to the question
- Amber – events and policies that have some relevance to the question
- Green – events and policies that are directly relevant to the question.

'The most significant event in the integration of the West Germany into Western Europe was its joining NATO in 1955.' How far do you agree?

1948	Marshall Plan applied to the Western zones
May 1949	Basic Law adopted
October 1949	West Germany joins the OEEC
1950	West Germany joins the Council of Europe
April 1951	West Germany joins the ECSC
1950–53	Korean War; West Germany asked to send forces
1953	Rising in East Berlin
1955	West Germany joins NATO
1955	Adenauer visits Moscow
1955	POWs return from Russia
1955	Plebiscite reincorporates Saar into West Germany
1957	West Germany joins the EEC

Now repeat the activity with the following questions:

To what extent was Germany treated as an international equal in the period 1949–63?

'Adenauer had more success in improving relations in the West than in the East.' How far do you agree?

Social change and the decline of Adenauer

Many Germans had co-operated with the Nazis. Adenauer's government needed to win their support, as democracy did not have widespread approval.

The impact of the Second World War

Cities had been damaged and property lost. Nearly 25 per cent of the population was fatherless, and women were forced out of work and back into the home because cheap labour was available from the Eastern zones. Refugees from the East numbered 12–13 million, and, along with *Gastarbeiter* (guest workers), they provided cheap labour.

Adenauer was able to win the support of those who lost their possessions in the war through the 1952 Equalisation of Burdens Act. This introduced a tax on property and funds not affected by the war and redistributed to those who had suffered the most.

Affluence

Adenauer created an affluent society and concentrated on 'building up' for the future. However, there was unequal distribution of wealth, and social inequalities resulted.

On the positive side, there were housing improvements: 430,000 houses were built by 1952, and 4 million by 1957. Wages had risen 400 per cent between 1949 and 1963; there was a ready availability of consumer goods and many people were travelling widely. Social welfare was available, with pensions and an insurance-based health and welfare system. These improvements ended any communist appeal and helped to create the image of the *Spiessbürger* (petty bourgeois), characteristic of the Federal Republic of Germany (**FRG**), with his cigar, car and new home in a rebuilt city.

There was little social change. The old **elites** still dominated. However, by the 1960s, new tensions emerged as economic growth lessened. There was growing electoral support for right-wing groups at a local level and unrest from the left, which was often led by the young, who had new cultural ideas.

Reintegration of former Nazis

Before the FRG was established, reintegration had occurred, and quickly, so that by the late 1940s, de-Nazification was meaningless. The government compensated those who had suffered, but exonerated most Nazis from their crimes. The need to care for war victims and refugees was balanced against responsibilities to the survivors.

Employing Nazis

Former Nazi civil servants regained the jobs they lost during de-Nazification through **Law 131**. As a result, 40–80 per cent of civil servants were ex-Nazis, and former Nazis continued working in the judiciary and universities. Pensions could be claimed for service to the Nazi state and this meant that former Nazis were not alienated. Even Adenauer employed a former Nazi as his personal adviser. The policies ensured that few felt shame or fear of retribution. However, in 1958, an office to investigate possible war crimes opened.

The decline of Adenauer

Adenauer's decline started with his handling of the decision not to run for president in 1959. His withdrawal damaged his image and reputation. This was reinforced further by his failure to intervene over the **Berlin Wall**.

In 1962, the weekly news magazine, *Der Spiegel*, criticised the readiness of German defence forces. When questioned on it, the defence minister misled the Bundestag. This was made worse as the government appeared to try to silence the magazine by raiding its offices and arresting some of the journalists. This provoked an outcry, as it appeared as if the government was acting like a dictatorship, and, ultimately, it resulted in Adenauer's resignation.

! Support or challenge?

Below is an exam-style question which asks you how far you agree with a specific statement. Below this are a series of general statements that are relevant to the question. Using your own knowledge and the information on the opposite page and the previous page, decide which general statements support or challenge the statement in the question and tick the appropriate box in each case.

'Adenauer's Germany was a continuation of the old Germany.' How far do you agree?

	Support	Challenge
Many old Nazis retained their jobs in the civil service, judiciary and universities.		
Economic policies saw a free market approach.		
Anti-democratic parties were banned to prevent them from wrecking democracy.		
The Der Spiegel affair showed that the government was still authoritarian.		
Women were forced back into the home, having to give up jobs.		
Adenauer pursued a policy of integration, not retribution, towards former Nazis.		
West Germany was integrated into Europe economically, politically and militarily.		
The powers of the president were largely formal and symbolic, preventing rule by decree.		
Support for right-wing groups at a local level was evident by the end of the period.		

⦿ Eliminate irrelevance

Below are a sample exam question and a paragraph written in answer to this question. Read the paragraph and, using the information from the opposite page, identify parts of the paragraph that are not directly relevant to the question. Draw a line through the information that is irrelevant and justify your deletions in the margin.

'Lack of social change was the main reason Adenauer lost support.' How far do you agree?

The lack of social change angered many on the left of German politics, who disliked the continued domination of the old elites. The situation was made worse by the lessening of economic growth in the early 1960s. Wages had risen some 400 per cent between 1949 and 1963, and consumer goods had become readily available, improving the standard of living. The right wing also made gains in local elections. The young also had new cultural ideas. This lack of social change also saw the emergence of the petty bourgeoisie, and that created resentment among those who had not made as much economic gain. The government also angered some by employing former Nazis, who continued to work in the judiciary, civil service and universities. The policies that the government adopted, such as Law 131, ensured that former Nazi civil servants regained the jobs they had lost during de-Nazification. In 1958, however, an office did open to investigate possible war crimes. Loss of support for Adenauer had begun in 1959, with his decision not to run for president, but really came to a head in 1962 with the Der Spiegel affair.

The emergence of the DDR

The division of Germany and the East German constitution

In 1948, Western representatives met in the **Parliamentary Council** and devised a constitution for a federal republic (FRG). The German Democratic Republic (DDR) was formed from the Soviet zone in October 1949, with a new constitution.

● The DDR constitution declared the state temporary, awaiting reunification.
● The parliament – **Volkskammer** – claimed to represent the people. It was not democratically elected and the number of seats for each party was allocated before the election.
● The upper house – **Länderkammer** – represented the five regions (this was abolished in 1958).
● The president – formal head of state – was Wilhelm Pieck.
● The prime minister – head of government – was Otto Grotewohl.

However, power remained with the Communist Party's general secretary (Ulbricht), the **Politburo**, central committee and local party units.

A 'state within a state' was established with the creation of the State Security Service (**Stasi**) in 1950, aided by the 'People's Police in Barracks' – regular police and border guards. There was greater surveillance and repression. *Länder* were abolished in 1952 and replaced with smaller units – *Bezirke* – which were easier for the party to control.

The 1953 rising

Events

On 16 June, workers on the Stalinallee, a prestige building project, demanded an end to increased working hours for no more pay. They called a general strike, which became political, as workers demanded the removal of Ulbricht and reunification with the West. Concerned about crushing the unrest and the unreliability of his own forces, Ulbricht called in Soviet troops. They dispersed the strikers, but unrest continued.

The causes

The rising was caused by a number of factors and was the culmination of long-term disquiet. The death of Stalin and the apparent promise of greater freedoms, with the announcement of the '**New Course**' in the Soviet Union, encouraged unrest. Ulbricht had already been summoned to Moscow and warned that his policies were causing disquiet because of:
● the tightening of border controls
● enforced **collectivisation** of agriculture
● government demands for increased productivity from workers, without an increase in pay
● Ulbricht's policy of 'Building of Socialism', which was announced in 1952 and increased the role of the state
● the failure of the government to persuade people of the need for changes.

Consequences

● The increase in working hours was ended and more consumer goods were to be produced to improve living standards.
● The SED (Communist Party) became more worried about potential unrest and adopted a harder line, increasing the powers and size of the Stasi.
● Ulbricht's power was strengthened.
● It became apparent that the West would not intervene to help.

Simple essay style

Below is a sample exam question. Use your own knowledge, the information on the opposite page and information from other sections of the book to produce a plan for this question. Choose four general points, and provide three pieces of specific information to support each general point. Once you have planned your essay, write the introduction and conclusion for the essay. The introduction should list the points to be discussed in the essay and outline the argument you intend to make. The conclusion should summarise the key points and justify which point was the most important.

Assess the reasons for the emergence of a separate East German state.

Turning assertion into argument ⓐ

Below are a sample question and a series of assertions. Read the exam question and then add a justification to each of the assertions to turn each one into an argument.

'The most important reason for the unrest in East Berlin in 1953 was the working conditions.' How far do you agree?

Government demands on workers played a major role in the unrest of 1953 because

_____

_____

However, it was Ulbricht's policy of 'Building of Socialism' which angered many because

_____

_____

This anger was reinforced by developments in the Soviet Union because

_____

_____

Economic change in the DDR

Land reform

Large estates had been given to peasants in 1945, but this created problems. They were unable to farm profitably, as they lacked resources and machinery. In 1952, the SED introduced collectivisation and formed 'land production co-operatives' (LPGs) as part of the plan for the 'Building of Socialism'. Mechanisation and the use of tractor-lending stations became possible, making agriculture more efficient. The policy was not popular with many, who abandoned their farms and fled to the West. This caused food shortages and a drop in production levels, which contributed to unrest in 1953.

By 1959, LPGs made up 45 per cent of the agricultural sector. By 1961, this figure was 85 per cent, but production had decreased further and rationing returned. This resulted in more people leaving, and was a major reason for the building of the Berlin Wall.

Industry and nationalisation

The 1950s

During the Allied occupation after the war, many large industries were placed under state ownership (nationalised). Most people worked in 'People's Own Factories' (*Volkseigene Betriebe*/VEBs), owned and managed by the state. The party set targets, handled discipline and ran social activities, all of which increased its control.

The emphasis was on heavy industry. Production targets, which were often unrealistic, were set in **Five Year Plans**, which were often changed and increased.

There was some upturn in the economy at the end of the 1950s.

Problems with the Five Year Plans

- Targets ignored consumer demands.
- An emphasis on quantity over quality reduced saleability.
- Plans were often out of date before they were implemented.
- Prices were fixed, but were not linked to supply and demand.
- Living standards improved slowly compared to the FRG. A metalworker earned less than 300 marks per month, whereas a manager earned 4,000 or even 15,000. Managers also received perks, such as cheap mortgages and separate canteens, all of which caused disquiet.

The Seven Year Plan

In 1959, a **Seven Year Plan** was implemented to align the economic development of the DDR with that of the Soviet Union. This plan brought in some consumer goods and improvements in living and working conditions. However, the consumer goods were expensive and not made in large enough quantities. Rationing did not end until 1958, another reason why many left for the West.

The 1960s

The Berlin Wall stabilised the workforce as there was less movement to the West. It also resulted in some economic freedoms, as there was less fear of losing workers. In 1962, the Seven Year Plan was abandoned because of economic problems. A new plan for 1962–70 was drawn up, but was never implemented.

However, a 'New Economic System for Planning and Direction' (NOSPL) was introduced in 1963. This system:

- brought more flexibility and input from workers
- allowed workers to share in profits, which encouraged production
- emphasised quality rather than quality.

These developments encouraged social change as the middle class left, often to go to the West.

! Complete the paragraph a

Below are a sample exam question and a paragraph written in answer to this question. The paragraph contains a point and specific examples, but lacks a concluding explanatory link back to the question. Using the information from the opposite page, complete the paragraph, adding this link in the space provided.

To what extent did the position of the workers improve in East Germany in the period 1949–63?

The opening of land production co-operatives and the resultant mechanisation, such as the tractor-lending stations, made the lives of farmers better and improved their efficiency. However, the introduction of collectivisation after 1952 was not popular with many, as they lost their land and this resulted in many abandoning their farms and moving to the West, causing food shortages and a fall in production levels, which helped contribute to the unrest in 1953. As the number of land production co-operatives continued to grow, food production continued to fall and rationing returned.

_____

_____

♦ Develop the detail a

Below are a sample exam question and a paragraph written in answer to this question. The paragraph contains a limited amount of detail. Annotate the paragraph to add additional detail to the answer.

How successful were the economic policies of the East German governments?

Industrially, the focus was on heavy industry, but there were many problems with the plans, which were unsuccessful. Wages were poor for workers compared with managers and that was unpopular, particularly as managers gained other benefits as well. There were attempts to improve the position for workers as more consumer goods were produced, but there were problems with this policy. Workers also suffered because of continued rationing. Food production decreased due to unpopular policies, and this made the position of workers even worse.

Social change in the DDR

There were opportunities for those who committed themselves to the new political system. Those who gained the most were peasants, the working class and women.

Peasants

- They gained land, but were later forced to join a collective.
- Farmers were given access to better machinery to work the farms.
- There was an increase in educational opportunities, particularly in higher education.

Factory workers

- As with the peasantry, workers were also given more opportunities for higher education.
- Promotion was available to workers who were loyal to the party. They were given the opportunity to manage factories.

Women

- Many became doctors.
- Women had increased support, with the provision of maternity care, crèches and after-school facilities to allow women to work part-time or at lower levels.

Mass organisations

The state established a number of mass organisations to give them control of all aspects of life. These included:

- Free German Trade Union League (FDGB) – established for workers, but the SED controlled its policies
- Democratic Women's League of Germany – the mass organisation for women
- League of Culture – had the support of many intellectuals who wanted to establish an anti-fascist state
- Society for Sports and Technology – organised sporting opportunities, but was also a preparation for military service
- German–Soviet Friendship Society – attempted to improve relations with Russia, and reinforced the idea that the Soviets had liberated Germany from fascism.

Youth education

The youth represented the future, and needed to be won over to communist views. Schools became comprehensive 'polytechnic' schools, with close links to industry or sport, and provided practical work experience. The SED controlled youth organisations. Scholarships were available for the disadvantaged, and university was opened up to all. Those from the professional and aristocratic classes were often discriminated against. Many left to study in the West.

Youth opposition

Not all were won over by state views. There was some support for Western culture, based around rock-and-roll music. The state response varied from clampdowns to tolerance.

Religion and the Churches

East German society was still religious. There were 15 million Protestants and 1 million Catholics. The SED wanted religion to wither away and fulfil **Karl Marx**'s prophecy that it was only the 'opiate of the people'. At first, the Church avoided the changes brought in by the SED:

- Church land was not seized.
- Ministers were not de-Nazified or removed from office.
- Churches ran their own internal affairs.

The situation changed in 1946 with the Law for the Democratisation of German Schools. This removed religious education from the curriculum. In 1952–53, there was a state campaign against Junge Gemeinde, the Protestant Youth Group. Members were prevented from remaining at school, taking their final exams and going to university. The campaign ended in June 1953.

Jugendweihe

In 1954, the Youth Dedication Service (*Jugendweihe*) was imposed on the young. This involved a commitment to Marxist views. As these contradicted Christian views, the service caused conflict. However, refusal resulted in discrimination at school and prevented post-compulsory education or a professional career. Churches were forced to change their view and accept that the dedication did not contradict Christian confirmation. This forced them into a relationship with the atheist state.

! Support or challenge? a

Below is a sample exam question which asks how far you agree with a specific statement. Below this are a series of general statements that are relevant to the question. Using your own knowledge and information on the opposite page, decide whether these statements support or challenge the statement in the question.

'Factory workers gained the most of any social group in East Germany from communist policies.' How far do you agree?

	Support	Challenge
Peasants gained land, but had to join collectives.		
A large number of mass organisations brought benefits to whole areas of society.		
There were opportunities for workers to gain an education.		
Women had many career opportunities available to them.		
Farmers had the chance of an education.		
Workers were able to manage factories.		
Education opportunities were available to the young and disadvantaged.		

ⓘ Develop the detail a

Below are a question and a paragraph written in answer to this question. The paragraph contains a limited amount of detail. Annotate the paragraph to add additional detail to the answer.

To what extent did communist rule bring about changes in East German society?

The advent of communist rule brought about increased opportunities for many groups in East German society who supported it. Loyal workers had increased social and economic opportunities, and women were able to play an increased role in society due to social provisions. The same was true of children from working-class backgrounds, as educational opportunities were provided for them. However, these gains must be balanced against the control the party had through mass organisations, which controlled a wide range of aspects of life.

The Berlin Wall

In the 1950s, many travelled from East to West Berlin. This increased in 1956, when the **Hungarian uprising** was crushed. Many left the East to escape repression.

In 1958, **Khrushchev** demanded that the Western powers recognise the DDR, withdraw from West Berlin and hand over access routes. The Soviets wanted to force the West to recognise the East German state, but the Allies ignored Khrushchev's demands.

The USA had poured large amounts of aid into West Berlin, and in comparison, East Berlin was not prosperous. Many left the East for West Berlin, including skilled and qualified workers, attracted to its freedom, cinemas, shops and better standard of living. The communists saw it as 'capitalist infection'. This exodus had a severe impact on the economy of the East, as well as undermining communism.

▼ Table 4.4 Number of people who left East Germany, 1949–61

Year	Number who left East Germany	Year	Number who left East Germany
1949	129,245	1956	279,189
1950	197,788	1957	261,622
1951	165,648	1958	204,092
1952	182,393	1959	143,917
1953	331,390	1960	199,188
1954	184,198	1961	159,730
1955	252,870	Total	2,691,270

The events of 1961

June

The Vienna Summit. Khrushchev pressurised US President Kennedy to withdraw Western forces from West Berlin within six months. Although inexperienced, Kennedy promised to protect freedom in West Berlin.

July 17

The West rejected Khrushchev's demands.

July 23

The East imposed strict travel restrictions. Up to 1,000 refugees had been leaving each day.

July 25

Kennedy gave further guarantees to West Berlin, and announced increased arms spending.

August 13

A barbed-wire barrier along the border between East and West Berlin was erected by East German soldiers, which ended free movement.

August 22

Barbed wire was replaced by a concrete wall. All routes to the West were closed, except **Checkpoint Charlie**.

October

US diplomats and troops crossed into the East, to test the Soviet reaction. On 27 October, Soviet tanks arrived at Checkpoint Charlie and refused to allow access to East Berlin. However, after this, there was a gradual pull-back of forces.

Consequences of the Berlin Wall

- Berlin was divided physically. Free access to the West was ended and families were divided.
- An exodus of workers was prevented. Those caught attempting to escape were shot.
- The workforce in the East was stabilised and economic progress in the East improved.
- The East introduced limited liberalisation and decentralisation, to win the support of the population.
- The Four Power Agreement on Berlin was ended.
- Kennedy refused proposals to pull down the Wall, and appeared weak.
- Khrushchev failed to remove the West from Berlin, and appeared weak.
- Tensions between the East and West increased, which encouraged the development of nuclear weapons.
- The building of the Wall was used as propaganda for the West. They argued that if communism was a workers' paradise, then why did the East have to stop people escaping?

Conclusion: What was the situation in East Germany at the end of the period?

- A totalitarian dictatorship had been established.
- Ulbricht, a hard-line **Stalinist**, had not followed the **de-Stalinisation** policies of the USSR.
- Ulbricht attempted to bring about **social justice**.
- Force and violence were not a regular part of life. They were seen more at the start and end of the period.

Support your judgement

Below are a sample exam question and two basic judgements. Read the exam question and the two judgements. Support the judgement that you agree with most strongly by adding a reason that justifies the judgement.

'The construction of the Berlin Wall was a disaster for Khrushchev and the East.' How far do you agree?

Overall, the construction of the Berlin Wall made Khrushchev and the East look weak.

_____

_____

_____

Overall, the construction of the Wall was a success for Khrushchev and the East.

_____

_____

_____

Developing an argument

Below are a sample exam question, a list of key points to be made in the essay, and a paragraph from the essay. Read the question, the key points and the sample paragraph. Using the information from the opposite page and from page 78, rewrite the paragraph in order to develop an argument. Your paragraph should explain why the factor discussed in the paragraph is either the most significant factor or less significant than another factor.

'The most important consequence of the Berlin Wall was an improvement in economic conditions in East Germany.' How far do you agree?

Key points:

- Reduction in the number of people leaving East Germany
- Increased tensions between the East and West
- It divided Berlin physically
- Economic progress in the East improved
- Khrushchev appeared weak, as the West did not leave Berlin
- Propaganda victory for the West

The construction of the Berlin Wall was particularly important in improving the economic position of East Germany. The Wall was built because in many years over 200,000 people had been leaving East Germany. The large numbers who left included skilled and qualified workers. Workers in the East thought that living conditions in the West were better and this made communism appear to be failing. The USA had given West Berlin a great deal of aid to rebuild, and the workers in East Berlin had seen the conditions in the West. In comparison to West Berlin, East Berlin was not prosperous and economic conditions were not as good. The building of the Wall prevented workers from leaving and those who tried to leave were shot. The Wall meant that Berlin was now divided physically, which had the result of dividing families. The Wall also meant that the workforce in the East became more stable and East Germany could bring in reforms which it hoped would win it support from the people. This was important for Khrushchev, as he had appeared weak by failing to drive the West out of Germany.

Exam focus

Below are a sample exam question and a model answer. Read the question, and then the answer and the comments around it.

How successful was Adenauer as Chancellor of West Germany in the period 1949–63?

Adenauer's long tenure of office and four electoral victories certainly seem to suggest that he was very successful. Certainly in terms of political dominance he was very successful, and it would also appear that in terms of both the economy and foreign policy, his period in office was one of almost unbroken success, as he brought the country political, economic and social stability. Perhaps it was only in the last years, with the *Der Spiegel* affair and his poor handling of the building of the Berlin Wall, that it could be argued that he was less successful.

> The opening paragraph offers a clear view of the line of argument that the candidate will take. It also offers a clear indication of the range of issues that will be covered.

After the failings of Weimar democracy, there were major concerns as to whether Adenauer would be able to achieve political stability in the new Federal Republic. Not only did he successfully ensure that democracy was established, but he presided over a period of political stability and ensured that there was no return to the unstable coalitions that had plagued Weimar. He was aided by the electoral system, which banned anti-democratic parties and combined proportional representation with constituency representation, but he was still skilful enough to retain liberal support for his CDU/CSU coalition after 1949, and win an overall majority in 1957, which was the first and only time a party has scored that level of success in the FRG. It could even be argued that he was almost too successful, as opposition was so weak that elections were little more than plebiscites in favour of Adenauer, and West German politics were transformed from a multi-party system to one of a 'vanishing opposition'. However, even this suggests that he must have pursued successful policies, as otherwise it was unlikely that such numbers would have voted for him. Most importantly, Adenauer prevented a return to 'Weimar' politics and unstable governments which lasted little more than eight months, and laid the foundations of democracy.

In many ways, the economic performance of West Germany was the most successful aspect of his period in office. He presided over a period of incredible economic growth, although credit should also be given to the economics minister, Ludwig Erhard, and his 'social market economy', which was helped by the fact that the German industrial base had not been as badly damaged by war as was first feared, and by money from Marshall Aid. Adenauer was also undoubtedly aided by conditions, particularly the Korean War, which stimulated demand for goods, and the flood of cheap labour from the East. However, no matter what the causes of this prosperity, Adenauer was viewed by many in West Germany as economically successful because annual growth rates averaged around 8 per cent, and as a consequence, there was large growth in average incomes. This resulted in a period of falling unemployment and rising living standards, which further added to his success, with improved industrial relations, as there were no longer struggles between workers and employers, but instead discussions as to how to divide up increased profits. It certainly appeared that the title of Erhard's book, *Prosperity for All*, had become a reality, and this further added to the impression of Adenauer's success.

> A good judgement is reached, with clever use of Erhard's book.

> There is a good range of supporting material throughout the paragraph.

In some ways, it could be argued that his success was seen even more clearly in his foreign policy with the West, although less so with the East. Unlike the period after the First World War, Adenauer was able to integrate Germany successfully into Western Europe and seal a rapprochement with France, which not only improved relations, but also, through the ECSC, helped to improve the German economy. Adenauer was able to make West Germany indispensable to Western powers, seen in the invitation to join NATO in 1955 – clear recognition that Adenauer had been able to get West Germany accepted as an equal and important partner in European stability. Adenauer was able to take West Germany into the OEEC and the EEC, which involved the country in successful moves towards economic integration with other Western powers.

However, Adenauer was less successful in his dealings with the Soviet Union. He refused to consider Stalin's supposed willingness to give up the DDR in favour of a united, but neutral Germany, and chose proactively to snub him, without exploring the possibility of unification further. This lack of response was also seen in 1953, when Adenauer ignored the Berlin uprising, and it would be repeated again with the construction of the Berlin Wall in 1961. However, it could be argued that he did not want to jeopardise his relationship with the West. Despite these events, he was successful in 1955 when he ignored the Hallstein Doctrine and visited Moscow to negotiate the return of thousands of German prisoners of war, who were still being held by the Soviets. Similarly, he was successful in overseeing the plebiscite which allowed the Saar to rejoin the FRG in 1957. However, the creation of a German army in 1955 did cause some anxiety at home among people who were still worried by the possibility of another war. Despite this, and his handling of the Berlin crises, his achievements in ensuring that West Germany was recognised as an equal partner and an accepted member of the community of nations were great, while the return of former prisoners also won him great popularity at home.

> There is a developed judgement at the end of the paragraph and it reflects what has been argued previously.

However, not only was his handling of the construction of the Berlin Wall less than successful, but his last years as chancellor were also marred by failure. The years after 1959 were less successful. Firstly, he harmed his reputation as an infallible politician by considering standing for the office of president and then withdrawing. With the Berlin Wall, he not only failed to intervene, but ignored the crisis and did not show sympathy, even postponing a visit to West Berlin for two days, with the result that when he turned up he was greeted with jeers. Finally, his treatment of the press in 1962 led to public outcry, as he attempted to silence *Der Spiegel* for its criticism of the readiness of West Germany's forces, in what some saw as a return to authoritarian dictatorship.

Despite the failings of the last years, Adenauer was very successful as chancellor. In three crucial areas he was particularly successful: he ensured democracy took root and political stability was achieved; he presided over unprecedented economic growth; and he restored West Germany's place in Europe after the war, all of which were in stark contrast to the Weimar democracy and its failings in these areas.

> The conclusion follows from the argument pursued in the main body of the essay. It picks up on the three areas that have been examined, and the comparison with Weimar emphasises the success.

The answer is well focused and wide-ranging. The level of supporting knowledge is very good and it is used to take the argument forward, rather than simply imparted. There are judgements about the issues discussed and an overall judgement is reached which follows from the argument in the main body of the essay. As a result, the answer would reach the higher levels of the mark bands.

Reverse engineering

You have now considered four sample high-level essays. Use these essays to make a bullet-pointed list of the characteristics of a strong Period Study essay. Use this list when planning and writing your own practice exam essays.

Exam focus

Below are a sample short-answer exam question and a model answer. Read the question, and then the answer and the comments around it.

Which was more important in ensuring stability in the Federal Republic in the years 1949–63?

- The Basic Law
- The economic miracle

The Basic Law, although not a constitution, because it was not permanent and could be amended when Germany was reunified, was important in bringing political stability to Germany. The Law helped to ensure that a democratic system, unlike the period after the First World War, would survive, as only political parties that upheld democracy were permitted and party pluralism was defined as essential. The Basic Law introduced mixed-member proportional representation with a 5 per cent hurdle in elections, and although this meant that there would be fewer parties in the Bundestag, it also meant that there would be more stability, as coalitions would be more stable. It was also important in creating stability, as the president was given only ceremonial powers, while the chancellor had to be elected and, unlike Weimar, where a simple vote of no confidence could bring down a government and destabilise the system, under the new constitution it could be brought down only by a constructive vote of no confidence, whereby the opposition would also have to be able to provide a stable majority to form a new government.

> The significance of the Basic Law is stated.

> A reason for its importance is stated and fully explained.

> A further reason for its importance is explained, and a useful comparison with Weimar is made to reinforce its significance.

The economic miracle helped to create stability within the Federal Republic as it created considerable prosperity for the workforce and created financial stability. As a consequence, living standards rose for large numbers of the population, and this made people content with the political and economic system, which was not the case under Weimar. Due to the increasing prosperity, many were willing to support Adenauer and the CDU, and this resulted in them voting for him in elections, with the result that he was even able to gain an overall majority in the 1957 election, and in the other elections was able to form strong coalitions that were able to sustain support in the Bundestag. Prosperity therefore led to a 'vanishing opposition', which further increased political stability. The prosperity also removed tensions between workers and employers, and allowed the government to introduce social reforms which benefited the workers and further encouraged them to support the government, rather than look for alternatives, as had happened during the Weimar period.

> The opening sentence introduces a key reason why the economic miracle should be seen as important.

> The importance of the factor is fully explained and supported with detailed knowledge.

> The response goes on to explain another reason why prosperity was important.

Both events were important in ensuring stability, as the Basic Law helped to bring about political stability and the economic miracle brought economic and financial stability. However, the economic miracle was more important because it also helped to create political stability, as it gave the new Federal Republic popular support and ensured that people would not look elsewhere for solutions; the new republic was able to solve quickly the economic problems the German people faced, and therefore win their loyalty. The Basic Law made it easier to counter the threat from extremist groups and uphold democracy, but the economic miracle ensured there was genuine support for the new republic.

> The opening sentence offers a judgement.

> That judgement is qualified and developed.

> The comparison in the final paragraph leads to an overall conclusion being reached.

The significance of the two issues is thoroughly analysed and explained, using detailed own knowledge. The final paragraph compares their importance in a balanced fashion before reaching an overall judgement. Although there is more that could be said, the answer reaches a convincing judgement in the time allowed and would reach the top level of marks.

Reverse engineering

In these short-answer essays there is a great deal of information that could be used, but does not appear in the response because of the constraints of time. Write your own response to this question, trying to use other knowledge of the events.

Glossary

25-point programme   Programme of the Nazi Party, drawn up by Hitler and Drexler, which saw the party change its name from the German Workers' Party.

Affidavit   Written statement that is confirmed on oath.

Anti-feminist ideology   Set of beliefs that women are inferior to men and play a subordinate role in society.

Anti-Semitism   Hostility towards or a dislike of Jews.

Armistice   Suspension of fighting before peace negotiations and a treaty. The armistice to end the First World War was signed on 11 November 1918.

Aryan   Nordic or Anglo-Saxon races that the Nazis believed were superior.

Asocial   Person demonstrating unacceptable behaviour.

Autarky   Self-sufficiency in terms of raw materials and food.

Authoritarian state   Strong, non-democratic government.

Auxiliaries   Those providing additional support for full-time members of the armed forces.

Balance of trade deficit   Importing more goods than are being exported.

Barter   System when goods are exchanged for other goods, rather than using money.

Basic Law   Constitution of West Germany established in 1949. It was to be temporary until there was a united Germany.

Bauhaus   New style of architecture and design in Weimar Germany.

Berlin Wall   Wall constructed in August 1961 by the communist powers to cut off East Berlin from the West, erected to prevent workers leaving the East as it was their last escape route.

Bezirke   Small, local units which replaced the five regions in East Germany in 1952.

Bizonia   Merged military zones of Britain and the USA.

Black market   Illegal trade in scarce goods.

Blitzkrieg   Lightning war: fast-moving divisions of tanks supported by planes and paratroopers to enable rapid advances.

Bomb plot   Attempt to assassinate Hitler on 20 July 1944. It involved both civilian resistance figures and army officers, including Colonel von Stauffenberg. He placed a bomb in a meeting room, but its movement before the meeting probably saved Hitler's life, and in the confusion afterwards, supporters of Hitler were able to arrest the conspirators.

Boycott   Refusing to deal with someone, in this case, refusing to shop in Jewish shops.

Bundesrat   Upper house of the West German parliament, which looked after the interests of the states.

Bundestag   Lower house of the West German parliament.

Capitalism   When industry and trade are controlled by private ownership.

Catholic Youth   Catholic Youth group, which was independent of Nazi control.

Chancellor   Head of government.

Chancellor democracy   Term used to describe the government of Adenauer. The constitution gave the chancellor the power to initiate policy. The chancellor is at the centre of the policy-making process.

Checkpoint Charlie   A crossing point between East and West Berlin that was the scene of a stand-off between US and Soviet tanks where they were just 100 metres apart.

Coalition   Government formed by the support of two or more parties in order to achieve a majority.

Cold War   Period of tension between the USA and the USSR, which lasted from 1945 until 1990, but did not result in open warfare.

Collectivisation   Combination of small, independent farms into a larger farm under state control.

Concordat   Agreement between Church and state.

Council of Europe   Early forerunner of the EEC, but without power.

Cult of personality   Using charisma and other personal qualities as a political leader to dominate the state.

DAF   German Labour Front, established by the Nazis in 1933 to replace independent trade unions. It helped to control the workers.

Dawes Plan   Introduced in April 1924 by the American banker, Charles Dawes, it did not reduce the reparations bill, but fixed payments for the first five years based on Germany's ability to pay, and spread payments over a longer period. It also made loans of 800 million gold marks to aid recovery.

DDR German Democratic Republic or East Germany (*Deutsche Demokratische Republik*).

Deficit financing Government funding spending by borrowing money.

Democratic centralism Decisions taken at the centre are passed down to the people. Views of the people should be influenced by the communist party and passed up to the centre.

De-Nazification Removal of former Nazis.

De-Stalinisation Policy followed by the Russian leader, Nikita Khrushchev. He denounced Stalin's policies as tyrannical at a meeting of the Communist International in 1956, which gave those in Eastern Europe greater freedom.

DNVP Right-wing nationalist party.

Dualism System of government where two political forces appear to govern the country, for example, the Nazi Party and the state.

Economic miracle Term used by historians to describe the economic recovery of West Germany after the Second World War.

ECSC European Coal and Steel Community, established to co-ordinate steel and coal production.

EEC Forerunner of the EU, established in 1957 and consisting of six member nations. Initially it was a customs union, allowing free movement of goods, capital and labour.

Einsatzgruppen SS units responsible for rounding up Jews and Communist Party officials.

Elites Conservative groups within German society who dominated the army, judiciary and civil service.

Emergency decree Rule by the president without using the Reichstag, using Article 48 of the Weimar Constitution.

Enabling Act Legal transfer of power to the Cabinet in Germany; it effectively gave Hitler full powers and created the dictatorship.

Ersatz Substitute products.

Ethnic Germans Pure-born Germans who shared a common culture.

EURATOM Set up to co-ordinate the development of nuclear energy in Western Europe.

Euthanasia Nazi programme of killing those too ill, old or handicapped to work.

Final solution Term used by the Nazis to describe the extermination of the Jews, begun in 1942.

First past the post Electoral system where the candidate who wins the most votes, not necessarily a majority, is elected.

Five Year Plans State plans and targets for economic development to be met in a five-year period.

Fixed income Income from savings or pensions, the value of which has declined due to inflation.

Four Year Plan Plan for the economy established by Göring in 1936, with the aim of increasing rearmament and making Germany self-sufficient.

Freikorps 'Free corps', right-wing former soldiers who acted as a paramilitary group and put down left-wing unrest.

FRG Federal Republic of Germany, or West Germany.

Gastarbeiter Overseas workers or guest workers, often from south-east Europe, who worked in West Germany, often for low rates of pay; they had no political rights.

Gauleiter Nazi official responsible for the administration of a province.

Genocide Organised murder of an ethic group.

German Workers' Party Despite its name, a small, right-wing party at the end of the First World War, which was anti-Semitic. It was led by Anton Drexler. Hitler joined, became its leader and changed it to the Nazi Party.

Gestapo Secret police.

Ghetto Area in a city inhabited by Jews. Under Nazi rule, Jews were separated from other citizens and lived in overcrowded conditions.

Gleichschaltung Co-ordination or bringing into line of people so that they act in the same way.

GNP Gross national product: the total value of all goods and services in a nation's economy.

Grammar school Selective school that followed a more academic curriculum than other Nazi schools.

Great Coalition Name given to Stresemann's coalition, formed in the 1923 election and made up of the SPD, DDP, Centre and DVP. It continued under Hermann Müller.

'Guns or butter' debate Debate on whether the priority should be rearmament or consumer goods.

Hallstein Doctrine West Germany would not formally recognise East Germany, and refused diplomatic relations with countries that did recognise East Germany as a separate state.

Herrenvolk   Racially dominant people who govern.

Hitler myth   Belief that Hitler could solve all of Germany's problems, that he was a superman.

Hitler Youth   Name for the range of youth groups under Nazi control. By 1939, membership was compulsory.

Hungarian uprising   Rising in 1956 which saw the Hungarian leader, Nagy, draw up plans for free elections and leaving the Warsaw Pact. Russian troops were sent in and there were two weeks of fighting before it was crushed. Nagy was executed.

Ideology   System of beliefs.

Indoctrinate   Teaching of a particular view so that it will be accepted and other views rejected.

Iron Curtain   Term used by Churchill to describe the divide between East and West.

Judiciary   System of courts in which judges administer justice.

Junkers   Landowning and aristocratic families, usually associated with the eastern areas of Germany.

Kaiser   Title given to the emperor of Germany, who ruled the country before 1918.

Kapp Putsch   Attempted right-wing coup, led by Wolfgang Kapp, the founder of the German Fatherland Party; he wanted to restore the Kaiser.

Korean War   War between North and South Korea, 1950–53. United Nations troops aided the South, while China aided the North.

Kripo   Criminal police within the Nazi state; they were often plain-clothed detectives who were concerned with serious crimes. They had offices in major towns and cities. They were under the control of the SS and were merged with the Gestapo.

Kristallnacht   Known as the Night of Broken Glass, it occurred on 9–10 November 1938. It saw the destruction of large numbers of Jewish businesses, shops and synagogues. The Nazis claimed it was in response to the assassination of the German ambassador in Paris by a Jew.

Labour exchange   Local office set up by the state where the unemployed went to find jobs.

Länder   Regional states of Germany.

Länderkammer   Upper house in the East German parliament, representing the five regions.

Law 131   Law introduced in 1951 as part of the German constitution which gave former Nazi civil servants the right to reinstatement in their former jobs.

League of Nations   International organisation set up after the First World War to resolve international disputes and social problems, the forerunner of the United Nations.

Lebensborn   'Spring of life', founded by Himmler to promote doctrines of racial purity.

London Conference   Conference of Western powers from February to June 1948 that agreed on a currency and the formation of the state of West Germany.

Marshall Aid/Plan   Plan proposed by the US General George Marshall, to give financial aid to nations in Europe to help them rebuild their economies and to stop the spread of communism.

Marxist-Leninist   Combination of beliefs in Marx's commitment to overthrow capitalism and Lenin's idea of the role of the party.

Mefo bill   Government money bill or credit note.

Mein Kampf   'My Struggle', the book written by Hitler while in jail after the Munich Putsch; it expresses his political views and ideas.

Nationalisation   State ownership of businesses.

NATO   North Atlantic Treaty Organization, a military agreement between many Western European states.

Nazi schools   The Nazis set up a number of specialist schools to produce the future elite, including a series of boarding schools run by the SS, Adolf Hitler Schools run by the Hitler Youth, and *Ordensburgen*, or finishing schools.

New Course   Plan to change the direction of Soviet policy after the death of Stalin in 1953.

New Order   Term to describe the economic, political and social integration of Europe under Nazi rule.

Oder–Neisse line   Border between East Germany and Poland, so-called because of the two rivers that formed the boundary.

OEEC   Organisation for European Economic Co-operation, made up of Western nations and receiving Marshall Aid. Aim was to rebuild the Western European economy.

Parliamentary Council   Established in 1948, this was the forerunner of the West German lower chamber in parliament. Its role was to draw up a constitution, the Basic Law, for West Germany, and it was then dissolved.

Patriotism   Love of one's country and being prepared to defend it.

Plebiscite   Vote by the people to decide a specific issue, similar to a referendum. A vote was held in 1935 to decide the future of the Saar, as had been agreed in the Treaty of Versailles.

Politburo Main executive body of Soviet government, responsible for defining and putting into practice government policy.

President Elected head of a republic.

Propaganda Information spread by political groups which is often exaggerated or biased.

Proportional representation Voting system where each party is represented in proportion to the number of votes they receive.

Putsch Violent rising or attempted seizure of power.

Racial genetics Belief that genetic characteristics were equated to race, and therefore the Aryan race must avoid contamination from other races so as to remain pure and strong to rebuild Germany.

Rationalisation Decree Order to ensure that existing resources were used efficiently.

Reichstag Parliament of Germany under the Reich, created in 1871.

Reparations Payments made by a defeated nation to compensate for the damage caused.

Rentenmark Currency introduced after the hyperinflation of 1923.

Rotfront Communist paramilitary organisation, the equivalent of the SA.

RSHA Reich Security Office, which brought together all the police and security organisations.

Ruhr Important industrial area of Germany, which produced large amounts of steel.

SA Brownshirts, so-called because of the colour of their uniform. They were known as the Stormtroopers and were established in 1921 under the leadership of Ernst Röhm.

Saar Area in Germany rich in coal and iron ore.

SD Intelligence branch of the SS.

Seven Year Plan Economic plan introduced in East Germany, giving greater flexibility and reintroducing the idea of profit.

Social Darwinism Belief that the world was a struggle between races and nations, influenced by the idea that only the fittest would survive.

Social justice A fair distribution of wealth and income, and social equality.

Spartacist Revolt Communist or revolutionary socialist revolt in Berlin in January 1919, crushed by the Freikorps.

SPD Left-of-centre Social Democratic Party.

Special-interest parties Parties that are formed to campaign on specific issues, such as compensation for losses during the hyperinflation.

Spiessbürger In West Germany, a 'petty bourgeois' who had gained from the improved standards of living created by the economic miracle.

SS Blackshirts, so-called because of the colour of their uniform. They were set up in 1925 as an elite bodyguard for Hitler, under the control of Himmler. They developed a reputation for obedience and loyalty.

'Stab-in-the-back' myth View that the German army had not lost the First World War, but had been betrayed by politicians and other forces at home such as socialists and Jews. This weakened the Weimar government.

Stalinist Supporter of Stalin's beliefs in centralisation and state control and his views of communism.

Stasi East German secret police.

Teutonic paganism Non-Christian beliefs of Germans from the past.

Total war A war that involves the entire population.

Totalitarian System of government where all power is centralised and there are no rival authorities.

Treaty of Brest-Litovsk Treaty signed with Bolshevik Russia in March 1918, allowing Germany to move all its troops to the Western Front and make a final push for victory.

Treaty of Rome Treaty establishing the European Economic Community, the forerunner of the EU.

Treaty of Versailles Treaty signed at the end of the First World War, declaring Germany guilty of starting the war. It caused much resentment within Germany that Hitler was able to exploit.

Trizonia Unified area of the three Western zones of Germany after the war, when France joined the British and US Bizonia.

Truman Doctrine US foreign policy which aimed to support governments fighting for 'freedom' against communism.

Unreliables Nazi term for those whose support for Nazism and its beliefs could not be trusted.

Untermenschen Racially inferior people.

Völkisch German term used to describe a policy based on the concept of race, to protect the superior German race from inferior races.

Volkseigene Betriebe 'People's Own Factories', but owned and managed by the state.

Volksgemeinschaft People's community, socially and racially united.

Waffen SS   Racially pure and fanatical units of the SS involved in the advances into Eastern Europe.

Wannsee Conference   Conference held in 1942 at which the final solution of the Jewish question in Europe was agreed.

Weimar   Town outside Berlin where the government of Germany met after the First World War because Berlin was too dangerous. The town gave its name to the Republic that was established after the war.

Welfare state   State protects the health and well-being of all of its citizens, particularly those in need.

Work-shy   Nazi term to describe those who the Nazis believed could work and contribute to the *Volk*, but would not work.

Young Plan   Signed in 1929, it further revised reparation payments, with the total sum reduced to £1,850 million, one-quarter of the original figure.

Key figures

Konrad Adenauer   A founder of the CDU and president of the Parliamentary Council, which drew up the foundations for West Germany. He was elected to the Reichstag in 1949 and became chancellor, a position he held until 1963, when he resigned. He was also foreign minister, 1951–55. He presided over a period of economic growth, political stability and the reintegration of West Germany into European affairs.

Martin Bormann   His first major job was to organise the Nazi Party and he was appointed Hitler's secretary in 1943. He was head of the party chancellery from 1941.

Heinrich Brüning   Leader of the Centre Party, the second largest party in the Reichstag, when he was appointed chancellor in 1930. However, his appointment was due to political intrigue, and his period in office lasted only until 1932. For much of the time he had to rule by decree, which some see as ending parliamentary government.

Anton Drexler   Violently anti-Semitic, at the end of the First World War he had established the German Workers' Party. This small party had little support, but this changed when Hitler joined and Drexler put him in charge of propaganda. Together, they drafted the 25-point programme and changed the name to the NSDAP.

Friedrich Ebert   Leader of the SPD, he was made chancellor of the provisional government when the Kaiser abdicated. He became the first president of the Weimar Republic in 1919 and remained in office until his death in 1925. He was a staunch supporter of the Republic and democracy.

Ludwig Erhard   Economic consultant in the Western zones after the war, becoming director of the economic council of Bizonia, overseeing currency reform. In 1949, he became minister of economics, a position he held in all Adenauer's governments. He wrote *Prosperity for All*, an influential book which outlined his belief in the free market, but with a social conscience. He played a significant role in the economic miracle.

Joseph Goebbels   Put in charge of Nazi propaganda in 1929, and from 1933 was minister of public enlightenment and propaganda. He issued the orders for the attacks on Jews on Kristallnacht, and in 1943 called for total war, following the defeat at Stalingrad. He committed suicide in 1945.

Hermann Göring   Involved in the Munich Putsch, he was a long-serving Nazi. He was a member of Hitler's first Cabinet, using the Reichstag fire to attack the communists and terror to impose Nazi power. He helped to organise the Night of the Long Knives and held a number of roles in the regime, including commander of the Luftwaffe and director of the Four Year Plan. He committed suicide before his execution at the Nuremberg trials.

Heinrich Himmler   Joined the Nazi Party in 1926 and was made head of the SS in 1929. He gradually took control of all the police forces in Germany. In 1943 he was made minister of the interior before being given senior roles in the army. He was captured by the British in 1945 and committed suicide.

Adolf Hitler   A corporal in the First World War, he joined the right-wing, anti-Jewish German Workers' Party after the war. He became its leader, changed its name to the National Socialist German Workers' Party (Nazi) and, as result of the Depression, turned it into the most popular party in Germany. Due to intrigue he became chancellor, turning his position into that of a dictator and attempting to establish a 1,000-year Reich.

Wolfgang Kapp   A Prussian civil servant, but also a nationalist, he helped to found the right-wing German Fatherland Party. He wanted to see a restoration of the Kaiser as leader of Germany and despised the Republic.

Nikita Khrushchev   Leader of the Soviet Union after Stalin.

Karl Marx   Nineteenth-century political thinker who provided the theoretical basis for communism. He argued that economic factors determined the course of history and that, ultimately, the workers would unite and throw off capitalism so that they were not exploited.

Pastor Martin Niemöller   U-boat commander and then a Protestant pastor. Although a nationalist, he soon opposed the Nazi regime and helped to establish the Confessional Church in 1934. He was arrested in 1937 for sermons critical of the Nazis and was held in concentration camps until the end of the war.

Ernst Röhm   Joined the Nazi Party in its early years, helped to establish the SA and became its leader. He was homosexual and it was this, along with a supposed plot by the SA against Hitler, that was used against him in the Night of the Long Knives, when he was arrested and killed.

Hjalmar Schacht   Experienced financier who had helped to set up the Rentenmark. He was president of the Reichsbank before being appointed minister of economics in 1934. He resigned as minister in 1937 and from the Reichsbank in 1939. He was arrested after the July bomb plot, but survived being held in a concentration camp.

Albert Speer An architect and close friend of Hitler, he was appointed minister of armaments in 1942 and oversaw a dramatic rise in production levels. However, he was unable to get the economy working at full potential. He was arrested after the war and sentenced to 20 years in jail.

Gustav Stresemann Founded the DVP in 1919. Initially opposed to Weimar, he changed his view, became chancellor in 1923 for 100 days, and was foreign minister from 1923 until his death in 1929. He wanted to see Versailles revised, but saw the best way was to work with the Allied powers, which brought a number of foreign policy successes.

Walter Ulbricht Fled Germany during the Nazi period, having been a member of the Communist Party. He returned with the Red Army, supported the foundation of the SED and was appointed its general secretary, thus becoming party leader. He held his position despite unrest because he was loyal to Moscow and through his use of party purges. He was largely responsible for the building of the Berlin Wall.

Paul von Hindenburg During the First World War he was field marshal and virtual dictator of Germany. At the end of the war he retired, but in 1925 was elected president, despite his lack of sympathy for Weimar. He was persuaded to appoint Hitler as chancellor in 1933 and remained in office until his death in 1934.

Franz von Papen A former officer in the cavalry, he became chancellor in 1932, but held the office for only a few months. He schemed to remove von Schleicher and appoint Hitler. He was vice chancellor to Hitler until his resignation following the Night of the Long Knives.

Kurt von Schleicher A professional soldier and civil servant. He had been defence minister in von Papen's government, but schemed for his removal and replaced him as chancellor until replaced by Hitler. He was killed during the Night of the Long Knives.

Horst Wessel Nazi stormtrooper killed in a fight with communists. A song he had written became a Nazi marching song.

Timeline

1918	March	Germany launches Spring or Ludendorff Offensive
	September	Ludendorff informs superiors war cannot be won
	November	Mutiny at Kiel
		Kaiser abdicates
		Armistice signed
1919	January	Spartacist uprising
	June	Treaty of Versailles signed
	July	Weimar constitution adopted
1920		Nazis announce 25-point programme
	March	Uprising in the Ruhr
		Kapp Putsch
1921		Hitler becomes leader of the Nazi Party
	August	Murder of Erzberger
1923	January	French and Belgian troops occupy the Ruhr
	January–November	Hyperinflation
	September	Stresemann forms the Great Coalition
	November	Munich Putsch
1924		Hitler writes *Mein Kampf*
	April	Dawes Plan
1925	April	Hindenburg elected president
	October	Locarno Treaties
1926		Germany joins the League of Nations
1927	January	Allied Disarmament Conference withdraws from Germany
	August	Allied troops withdraw from garrisons in the Rhineland
1928	May	Müller's Grand Coalition formed
1929	Spring	Unemployment at 2.5 million
	June	Young Plan proposed
	October	Death of Gustav Stresemann
		Wall Street Crash
1930	March	Brüning replaces Müller as chancellor
	September	Nazis make large gains in elections to the Reichstag
1931	July	Failure of major banks in Germany
1932	January	Unemployment reaches 6.1 million
	May	Von Papen replaces Brüning as chancellor
	July	Elections to the Reichstag; Nazis the largest party
	November	Elections to the Reichstag; Nazi support falls
	December	Von Schleicher replaces von Papen as chancellor
1933	January	Von Schleicher dismissed as chancellor
		Hitler appointed chancellor
	February	Reichstag fire
	March	Elections
		Enabling Act
		Establishment of concentration camps, originally for political prisoners
	April	Boycott of Jewish businesses
	July	One-party state established
		Concordat signed with papacy
		Sterilisation Law
1934		Confessional Church established to resist Nazi control of Protestant Churches
		Night of the Long Knives removes the SA from influence
		Death of Hindenburg; Hitler combines offices of chancellor and president; army swears oath of loyalty to Hitler
1935		Nuremberg Race Laws
		Ministry of Church Affairs established to co-ordinate Protestant Churches
		Introduction of *Lebensborn* to 'improve racial quality'
		Mass arrests of socialists and communists by Gestapo
1936		Göring introduces Four Year Plan to help preparations for war
1937		Nazi relaxation of policy towards women as they are needed as workers
1938		Decree for the Struggle against the Gypsy Plague
		Kristallnacht, attacks on Jewish property and synagogues
1939		Joining the Hitler Youth becomes compulsory
		Euthanasia campaign started
1941		Bishop Galen's sermon against euthanasia
1942		Wannsee Conference agrees on the final solution for the Jewish problem
1944		Stauffenberg bomb plot
		Execution of Edelweiss Pirates in Cologne
1945		Yalta Conference

	April	Death of Hitler
	May	Surrender of Germany
	August	Potsdam Conference
1946		Formation of Socialist Unity Party in Eastern zone of Germany following merger of KPD and SPD
		Law for democratisation of German schools removes Religious Studies from East German education system
1947		Formation of Bizonia following merger of US and British zones
		Truman Doctrine announced by US President, offering support to nations fighting communism
		Marshall Plan offers aid to Europe
1948		Currency reform in Western zones, followed by reform in Eastern zone
		Berlin blockade starts
		Western representatives meet to discuss constitution for new democratic Western German state
1949		Formation of Trizonia as France joins Bizonia
		Berlin blockade ends
	May	West Germany (Federal Republic) comes into existence
	August	Adenauer elected Chancellor of West Germany
		West Germany joins Organisation for European Economic Co-operation
	October	East Germany (Democratic Republic) comes into existence
1950		Creation of Stasi in East Germany
		Outbreak of Korean War
1951		West Germany joins European Coal and Steel Community
1952		First series of collectivisation in East Germany
		SRP outlawed in West Germany
		Stalin's notes suggesting unification of Germany
1953		Death of Stalin
		Berlin rising
		5 per cent hurdle introduced for elections in West Germany
		Adenauer wins second election
1954		Youth Dedication Service reintroduced and imposed in East Germany
1955		West Germany joins NATO
		Warsaw Pact established as a response to NATO
		KPD outlawed in West Germany
		Adenauer visits Moscow and secures return of former POWs
		Recreation of West German army
1956		Hungarian uprising
1957		Adenauer wins third election with overall majority
		Establishment of European Economic Community
		Saar plebiscite returns the area to West Germany
		CDU renounces Ahlen Programme
		West Germany joins EURATOM
1959		Bad Godesberg Programme adopted by SPD in West Germany
1960		Second wave of collectivisation in East Germany
1961		Building of Berlin Wall
		Adenauer wins fourth victory, but with a reduction in number of seats
1962		*Der Spiegel* affair
1963		Resignation of Adenauer
		New Economic System for Planning and Direction introduced in East Germany

Answers

Section 1

Page 11, Turning assertion into argument

The Treaty of Versailles was harsh on Germany economically and territorially because it lost large amounts of land that were rich in raw materials, such as Upper Silesia, and because Germany was divided in two.

However, it did not completely reduce Germany's influence in Europe because many of the new states in Central Europe were very weak.

Nevertheless, it was still a cause of bitterness as Germany was blamed for the start of the war and had to accept war guilt.

Page 11, Delete as applicable

It is **unfair** to argue that the Treaty of Versailles did little damage to Germany. The territorial losses were **great** and had **great** impact on the economy. It did mean that **some** Germans were now living outside the borders of Germany. In some ways, the loss of colonies had a **lesser** impact on the economy. However, the government **lost** support for signing the treaty and this would make it **harder** for it to survive the challenges it faced. It was not just the loss of land that the government had to deal with, but military issues. The military reductions had **great impact** as Germany felt **insecure** from the threat from France. In this way, to a **great** extent, Versailles was damaging for Germany.

Page 15, Develop the detail

Between 1924 and 1929, the Weimar government was largely successful **in achieving political and economic stability**. The government was able to bring about some economic recovery **with production levels returning to those of before the war**, although the recovery was not complete and depended on help from outside the country, **particularly loans from America**. Conditions for workers also improved and they gained many benefits, **as the number of hours they had to work were reduced to eight, and pensions and unemployment benefit were also provided**. The political situation was also more stable, **with the establishment of the Grand Coalition**, and support for extreme parties, **such as the Nazis,** fell**, so that they won only 12 seats in 1928**, and support for those that supported democracy increased. Foreign policy was also a success, **with Germany signing both the Dawes Plan and the Locarno Treaties**, although some **nationalist** groups were angered by the agreements. However, Stresemann did improve relations with European powers and Germany was able to join international organisations, **such as the League of Nations**.

Page 17, Develop the detail

The impact of the Great Depression in Germany was particularly severe because it led to loans **from America which had funded the recovery** being recalled and the economy needed these to survive. As a result, many people became unemployed, **with numbers reaching 6 million by January 1932**, and this had an impact on the political situation, as they lost faith in the government and looked to other parties to solve their problems. **Many turned to the extremist parties, the Nazis and communists, with the Nazis winning 107 seats in July 1930**. The government was weakened as the Depression created policy divisions within it, **most notably over the issue of unemployment benefit**. The government was also seen as weak because it could not control the country. The collapse of the government led to the appointment of a more right-wing chancellor, **Heinrich Brüning**, and his method of government **in dissolving the Reichstag and ruling by emergency decree** suggested that democracy could not deal with the problems Germany faced, encouraging support for other parties.

Page 21, Support or challenge?

	Support	Challenge
Hitler's appointment as chancellor was the result of constitutional procedures.		X
Nazi support was in decline and therefore they had to seize power.	X	
It was electoral support that brought Hitler to power.		X
Intrigue, rather than seizure of power, best describes Hitler's appointment as chancellor.		X
Rather than seizing power, other figures believed they were using Hitler.		X
Hitler came to power only because Hindenburg and von Papen had been unable to establish an authoritarian government.		X
Hitler came to power because he demanded that he was appointed chancellor because the Nazis were the largest party.	X	

	Support	Challenge
Hitler's dislike of democracy resulted in the events of January 1933 being called a seizure of power.		X
Hitler and the Nazi Party came to power because of their electoral strength.		X

Section 2

Page 29, Delete as applicable

Hitler was to a **fair** extent only ever a weak dictator. This is because he **sometimes** relied on subordinates to put his will into practice, as he was **never** interested in the day-to-day running of the government. This situation was reinforced as Hitler **sometimes** had contact with ministers and therefore they followed the policy of 'working towards the Führer'. War ensured that these issues **grew** as Hitler **did not allow** the Cabinet to meet. However, Hitler **always** made decisions about foreign policy.

Page 29, Identify an argument

Answer 2 is the argument.

Page 31, Turning assertion into argument

Propaganda played a significant role in gaining the Nazi Party popular support because **it was difficult to escape from the propaganda as it was present in all aspects of life**.

However, the success of propaganda depended on its purpose as **it was less successful in creating a new culture**.

Yet it did do much to strengthen the Hitler myth because **it reinforced the view that Hitler was all-powerful and able to solve all problems**.

Page 33, Develop the detail

The Nazi state had a variety of groups, **such as the courts, the SS and the Gestapo**, with which to enforce its will on the people of Germany. The courts played a crucial role in this and could usually be relied on to implement Nazi wishes because of the reforms that had been made to them **in 1939, with those who opposed Nazi beliefs removed and those who remained studying Nazi beliefs**. The SS probably played the most important role in the organisation of terror, with its range of activities, **responsible for security, ideology and race, the economy and a variety of military issues**. It had a number of roles, **including intelligence gathering, policing and military functions**, and this grew when the Second World War broke out. It ran the concentration camps and the Nazis used these to attack political opponents, **such as communists and**

socialists and those who did not fit their ideal, **such as homosexuals, beggars, gypsies and asocials**, with the numbers in the camps growing dramatically, **from 25,000 at the start of the war to some three-quarters of a million by 1942**. Although the Gestapo was feared by many Germans, it was actually small, **with only 20,000–40,000 agents**; it was the block wardens who were the important element in imposing Nazi will at a local level.

Page 35, Support or challenge?

	Support	Challenge
Gestapo numbers were limited and this made opposition much easier.		X
Opposition lacked organisation and this made it weak.	X	
Most people simply accepted the regime and were happy they had work.	X	
Opposition groups continued to exist throughout the period.		X
Pamphlets that opposition groups produced had little impact.	X	
People were too frightened to listen to messages of opposition.	X	
There were a large number of different opposition groups.		X
The left wing provided the most effective opposition to the Nazis.	X	
Defeats in the war increased opposition to the regime.		X

Page 35, Developing an argument

The Churches opposed some of the Nazi policies. Bishop Galen of Münster opposed the policy of euthanasia and was able to force the government to abandon the policy temporarily. Other Church leaders, such as Bonhoeffer, were sent to concentration camps because of their opposition. **Church leaders were therefore able to halt some of the Nazi policies, while even their sermons must have had an impact, as despite the popularity of the Church leaders, the Nazis were forced into silencing them**. There was also opposition from youth groups and students. Youth groups, such as the Edelweiss Pirates and the Swing Youth, opposed the Nazis by playing jazz music, while student groups such as the White Rose produced pamphlets attacking the Nazis; **however, such opposition had little real impact and did not prevent the Nazis from continuing their policies**. As the war progressed, some of the army began to oppose Hitler. The opposition had been slow to develop because of the early military success, but after defeat at Stalingrad it developed and culminated in the Stauffenberg plot, which attempted to kill Hitler. **However, the failure of the plot and the slowness of officers to act allowed the regime to recover.** Political parties had been banned and largely destroyed by 1934, but they did go underground and produce pamphlets attacking the regime. However, their main concern was simply to survive, **and with the divisions between the communists and the SPD, they represented little threat to the regime.**

Page 37, Develop the detail

The Churches were quite successful in resisting Nazi policies, **forcing them to abandon policies such as euthanasia.** Although, some Protestant Churches supported the Nazis **as they liked their emphasis on the family**, and helped the Nazis, **allowing them to use churches for meetings.** However, the attempt to reorganise the Protestant Churches **under the German Faith Movement** failed, **with only 5 per cent of the population joining**, and other Protestant leaders did resist and established their own Church, **the Confessional Church under Pastor Niemöller**, independent of the state. The Catholic Church wanted its independence and reached an agreement with the regime, **signing the Concordat in July 1933**, but later the Nazis attempted to ignore the concessions. To overcome the problems, the Nazis tried to establish an alternative to Christianity, **the German Faith Movement, a form of teutonic paganism**, but this also failed. Policies to undermine the Church were also adopted by the Nazis – **they closed some Church schools, removed crucifixes from others, banned nativity plays and carols from schools and undermined Catholic Youth groups** – but it was hard for the Nazis to take much action and their policies had only limited success.

Page 39, Spot the mistake

There is no argument. The paragraph describes the economic policies without explaining whether they were successful or not.

Page 39, Turning assertion into argument

The German economy was not prepared for a long war in 1939 because **it was still reliant on importing raw materials and was not self-sufficient.**

However, the Four Year Plan under Göring did help to overcome some problems because **production in some industries, such as aluminium, increased.**

Despite this success, there were still problems because **it did not reach the targets for oil or rubber and failed to meet the levels required by the armed forces.**

Page 41, Complete the paragraph

As a result, Nazi policies can be seen as a failure as they had to abandon their ideals about women so that their war aims could be achieved.

Page 41, Develop the detail

In order to achieve their goal of a larger population, women were expected to have large families. In order to achieve this, the Nazis introduced incentives for women to marry, **with interest-free loans of up to 600 Reichsmarks if they also gave up work**, and offered benefits if they had large numbers of children, **by offering marriage loans and tax reductions for each child.** At the same time, a propaganda campaign raised the status of motherhood, and further rewards were given to women depending on the number of children they had, **through the Mother's Cross.** However, whether some of the measures to increase the size of families should be seen as bringing benefits is a matter of debate, **as divorce and anti-abortion laws were made stricter.** Although the woman's role was seen as different to that of men, the Nazis argued that they improved women's status, **as the Nazis emphasised the importance of motherhood based on Kinder, Küche, Kirche.** However, many would argue that they were denied many opportunities, **as labour exchanges were instructed to favour men and educational opportunities for women were limited.**

Page 43, Support or challenge?

	Support	Challenge
There was great deal of emphasis on PE in the Nazi curriculum.	X	
Girls were taught the importance of being healthy.		X
Racial studies formed a key part of the Nazi curriculum.		X
In the Hitler Youth, much time was devoted to marching, camping and hiking.	X	
History lessons were largely about German history from the First World War.		X
Nazi ideology was taught in both schools and the Hitler Youth.		X
Maths lessons were often based around the angles of missiles and projectiles or the bombing of Jewish ghettoes.	X	
Religious education was dropped from the curriculum.	X	
The Nazis allowed the Catholic Youth movement to survive.		X

Page 45, Eliminate irrelevance

It could be argued that many of the Nazi policies towards the Jews in this period were popular. They were, after all, only exploiting the Germans' desire for a scapegoat for their problems, particularly defeat in the First World War and the economic crisis. However, some policies, such as the euthanasia programme aimed at the mentally ill, provoked criticism from Church leaders and were abandoned. The popularity of the policies can be seen in events such as Kristallnacht, when, according to many accounts, there was a spontaneous attack on Jewish homes, businesses and synagogues. However, in contrast, the policies adopted during the Second World War were not always popular, with many ordinary Germans sheltering Jews, even if members of the SS were willing to commit atrocities. Yet the lack of support for events such as the boycott of Jewish businesses in April 1933 suggests that even those policies were not popular, and that policies were simply accepted because people were forced to conform or were subject to propaganda.

Section 3

Page 51, Develop the detail

The early victories in the war suggested that the German economy was well prepared for war. Hitler had been determined to avoid the problems faced by Germany in the First World War, and therefore prepared thoroughly for all aspects of war production: **with decrees issued in December 1939, military expenditure was doubled in the period 1939–41, and food and clothes rationing was brought in soon after the start of war**. Despite this, the policy was not successful in a number of ways as **armaments production was low** and economic mobilisation was limited, **reflected in the slow increase in the number of tanks and planes produced**. The problems were made worse by organisational issues, which meant there were groups, **such as the Ministries of Finance, Armaments, Labour and Economics**, with different interests. In the period when Speer first came to power, however, there appeared to be an improvement, and war production rose until later in the war, **tank production rising 25 per cent and ammunition production 97 per cent**. However, the levels could have been even higher, but were limited by a number of factors, **such as the demands of the SS and *Gauleiters*, as well as the failure to fully exploit conquered territories**, with production peaking in June 1944, but never reaching its potential.

Page 55, Turning assertion into argument

Economic policies were a significant method of winning popular support because they led to **the seizure of large estates and their redistribution**.

However, in many instances, the Soviets were more concerned with exploiting their zone economically because **they had suffered a great deal of damage in the war and wanted reparations from Germany**.

Also, Russia took away technical experts to Russia because **they wanted to catch up with the West and were technologically behind**.

Page 57, Support or challenge?

	Support	Challenge
Elections were to be held in Germany, starting at local level.		X
A range of political parties were established in the Russian zone.		X
Communists were to be in charge of personnel and education.	X	
Not all mayors were communists.		X
All parties were brought together in a 'National Front'.		X
Mass organisations were put under communist control.	X	
Liberal and religious parties were allowed.		X
The Soviet military command suppressed political party activity in Berlin.	X	
The National Democratic Party and the Democratic Peasants Party of Germany were established.		X

Page 57, Developing an argument

The control of key appointments was a factor in enabling the communists to dominate the Soviet zone. The communists did control education, **as this was seen as a key long-term area to control**. The control of education meant that the young would be educated in communist beliefs **and therefore become loyal supporters of the regime**. The communists also controlled the appointment of key personnel, **as this would help them to build up control over key areas**. The appointment of key personnel gave the communists a group of reliable supporters in important areas. The communists also established mass organisations for women, trade unions and young people, **which meant that the communists would be able to influence the social life of workers and peasants**. The SED also won popular support because of its economic policies, as the property of factory owners, former Nazis and landowners was seized, **and this was popular with workers and** peasants, who often gained land or the chance to become managers in factories.

Page 59, Support or challenge?

	Support	Challenge
There were severe food and fuel shortages in the Western zone.	X	
There had been a large influx of refugees from the East.		X
The Western zone had suffered large-scale damage during the war.	X	
The new government had to overcome the impact of Nazi rule and genocide.		X
The structure of the ACC and the need to achieve unanimous decisions created difficulties.		X
There were divisions between France, the USA and Great Britain.		X
The weakness of the British economy meant the British were unable to support their zone.	X	
The weakness of the German currency and the resultant black market created economic problems.	X	
Inflation severely damaged the economy in the Western zone.	X	

Page 59, Delete as applicable

To a **great** extent, economic problems were the greatest difficulty facing the Western zones in the period 1945–49. **Most** of the economic difficulties were due to the legacy of the Second World War. This was particularly true with issues such as food shortages and homelessness. These problems lasted a **long** time and were made worse by difficulties in Britain, which could not fund its zone. These problems got **worse** by 1947 and **challenge** the view that it was difficulties from the war that were the main issue. The situation was also **not helped** by the attitude of **France and Russia**. To a **great** extent, the economic problems were overcome only when Trizonia was formed and a new currency introduced. However, it was the attitude of Russia towards the Western zones that was the greatest problem for the Western zones because

Page 61, Turning assertion into argument

The actions of the Western powers within their zone were to blame for the Berlin blockade because **of**

the introduction of the Truman Doctrine and Marshall Aid.

However, the East precipitated the action because **of its desire to expand westward and take the whole of Berlin**.

Also the East's attitude towards currency reform was crucial because **it refused to co-operate with the West over its reform so that the black market could end and a stable currency that would allow economic reform could be introduced**.

Section 4

Page 67, Develop the detail

There were many elements of the Basic Law, **such as combining PR with first past the post and an agreement that all parties would uphold democracy, and the indirect election of the president to ensure that he was a supporter of democracy**, that were designed to prevent a repeat of 1932–33. Political parties had to support the system and those that did not, **such as the KPD and SRP**, were banned. The president was not voted for by the people, **but elected indirectly**, and his powers were limited. The chancellor had to be approved by parliament and could not simply be dismissed by the president. The voting system was designed to prevent small parties from being represented – **they had to gain 5 per cent of the vote** – and the combination of two electoral systems **of PR and first past the post** also ensured that more extreme parties were unlikely to gain seats.

Page 69, Turning assertion into argument

It could be argued that popular self-government disappeared in Germany under Adenauer because **the number of political parties declined**.

However, the period can also be described as chancellor democracy because **of the control and power he had over the government**.

Yet elections could be seen as irrelevant because **they were little more than plebiscites on his government**.

Page 71, Delete as applicable

To a **fair** extent it was the economic policies introduced before 1949 that brought about the West German economic recovery. **Most** of the policies helped to stimulate the economy, and a reduction in taxes helped as people had **more** to spend on goods, which **encouraged** production. These policies **encouraged** people to work and this was seen in a **decrease** in absenteeism. However, it was not just the decisions made before 1949 that were important, as the Korean War played a crucial role because

Page 73, Develop the detail

Adenauer's attempts at integration were successful. He was able to convince European powers of his peaceful intentions and achieved a good relationship with his Western neighbours, **particularly France**, through various European organisations, **including the OEEC**, acknowledged in his recovery of lost land, **with the Saar regained in 1957**. West Germany was at the forefront of many European organisations designed to bring about economic integration, **such as the ECSC and the EEC**, and later political organisations, **such as the European Council**. The country became trusted militarily and developed its own forces. However, these achievements were at the expense of better relations with the East, although there were some successes, **with the return of former POWs from Russia in 1957**. Adenauer would not recognise a divided Germany, **upholding the Hallstein Doctrine**, and gave little support to those Germans cut off from West Germany.

Page 75, Support or challenge?

	Support	Challenge
Many old Nazis retained their jobs in the civil service, judiciary and universities.	X	
Economic policies saw a free market approach.		X
Anti-democratic parties were banned to prevent them from wrecking democracy.		X
The *Der Spiegel* affair showed that the government was still authoritarian.	X	
Women were forced back into the home, having to give up jobs.	X	
Adenauer pursued a policy of integration, not retribution, towards former Nazis.	X	
West Germany was integrated into Europe economically, politically and militarily.		X
The powers of the president were largely formal and symbolic, preventing rule by decree.		X
Support for right-wing groups at a local level was evident by the end of the period.	X	

Page 75, Eliminate irrelevance

The lack of social change angered many on the left of German politics, who disliked the continued domination of the old elites. ~~The situation was made worse by the lessening of economic growth in the early 1960s. Wages had risen some 400 per cent between 1949 and 1963, and consumer goods had become readily available, improving the standard of living. The right wing also made gains in local elections. The young also had new cultural ideas.~~ This lack of social change also saw the emergence of the petty bourgeois, and that created resentment among those who had not made as much economic gain. The government also angered some by employing former Nazis, who continued to work in the judiciary, civil service and universities. The policies that the government adopted, such as Law 131, ensured that former Nazi civil servants regained the jobs they had lost during de-Nazification. In 1958, however, an office did open to investigate possible war crimes. ~~Loss of support for Adenauer had begun in 1959, with his decision not to run for president, but really came to a head in 1962 with the Der Spiegel affair.~~

Page 77, Turning assertion into argument

Government demands on workers played a major role in the unrest of 1953 because **the government demanded that workers worked longer hours but for no more pay**.

However, it was Ulbricht's policy of 'Building of Socialism' which angered many because **it increased state control**.

This anger was reinforced by developments in the Soviet Union because **in Russia the death of Stalin had led to the promise of greater freedoms**.

Page 79, Complete the paragraph

As a result, the position of workers did not improve, as the fall in agricultural production meant there was less food available for the workers.

Page 79, Develop the detail

Industrially, the focus was on heavy industry, **with the government setting production targets in its Five Year Plans**, but there were many problems with the plans, which were unsuccessful. **Consumer needs were ignored and the emphasis was placed on quantity rather than quality.** Wages were poor for workers compared with managers, **with the latter earning 4,000 marks per month compared with the worker's 300**, and that was unpopular, particularly as managers gained other benefits as well, **such as cheap mortgages and separate canteens**. There were attempts to improve the position of workers, as more consumer goods were produced, but there were problems with this policy, **as the goods were expensive and not enough were made**. Workers also suffered because of continued rationing, **which did not end until 1958**. Food production decreased due to unpopular policies, **such as collectivisation**, and this made the position of workers even worse.

Page 81, Support or challenge?

	Support	Challenge
Peasants gained land, but had to join collectives.		X
A large number of mass organisations brought benefits to whole areas of society.		X
There were opportunities for workers to gain an education.	X	
Women had many career opportunities available to them.		X
Farmers had the chance of an education.		X
Workers were able to manage factories.	X	
Education opportunities were available to the young and disadvantaged.		X

Page 81, Develop the detail

The advent of communist rule brought about increased opportunities for many groups in East German society who supported it, **such as peasants and factory workers**. Loyal workers had increased social and economic opportunities, **such as better education and management opportunities and better machinery**, and women were able to play an increased role in society due to social provisions, **such as improved maternity care, crèches and after-school facilities**. The same was true of children from working-class backgrounds, as educational opportunities, **such as scholarships and university opportunities**, were provided for them. However, these gains must be balanced against the control the party had through mass organisations, **such as the Democratic Women's League of Germany or the Society for Sport and Technology**, which controlled a wide range of aspects of life.

Page 83, Developing an argument

The construction of the Berlin Wall was particularly important in improving the economic position of East Germany. The Wall was built because in many years over 200,000 people had been leaving East Germany, **which had a serious impact on the East German economy**. The large numbers who left included skilled or qualified workers, **who were the very workers East Germany needed if it was to improve its economic performance and technological developments**. Workers in the East thought that living conditions in the West were better, and this made communism appear to be failing **and encouraged them to take their talents to the West, which was a great propaganda victory for the West**. The USA had given West Berlin a great deal of aid to rebuild, and the workers in East Berlin had seen the conditions in the West **and therefore wanted to flee**. In comparison to West Berlin, East Berlin was not prosperous and economic conditions were not as good. The building of the Wall prevented workers from leaving and those who tried to leave were shot. The Wall meant that Berlin was now divided physically, which had the result of dividing families; **although it did mean that the loss of workers was finally stopped, the need for the Wall was exploited for propaganda by the West**. The Wall also meant that the workforce in the East became more stable and East Germany could bring in reforms which it hoped would win it support from the people, **and make the East more appealing to them**. This was important for Khrushchev, as he had appeared weak by failing to drive the West out of Germany, **and because communism had become unpopular with many in the East because of the poor economic conditions**.